Miracles and Wonders from the King of Kings and Lord of Lords

Miracles and Wonders from the King of Kings and Lord of Lords

The Journey of Han Fu in China

Harry Winslow

RESOURCE *Publications* · Eugene, Oregon

MIRACLES AND WONDERS FROM THE KING OF KINGS AND
LORD OF LORDS
The Journey of Han Fu in China

Resource Publications
An Imprint of Wipf and Stock Publishers
199 W. 8th Ave., Suite 3
Eugene, OR 97401

www.wipfandstock.com

PAPERBACK ISBN: 979-8-3852-2424-1
HARDCOVER ISBN: 979-8-3852-2425-8
EBOOK ISBN: 979-8-3852-2426-5

VERSION NUMBER 01/20/26

Dedicated
to
my loving wife and four sons
Ruth, Glenn, Mark, Keith, Rodney,
who are such an integral part of my journey.

Dedication

Contents

Preface

The Power of a Name

I WAS BORN IN 1938 in Henan Province, China, where my American parents had gone to work as missionaries. A Chinese scholar, Professor Ho, held me as a tiny baby in his arms and gave me my Chinese personal name 漢復 *Han Fu*. These two characters have a great deal of meaning. Because of the magnificent Han Dynasty, 漢 *han* stands for "the Chinese people." 復 *fu* means "to return." Put together, 漢復 *Han Fu* means "the Chinese people return." Professor Ho blessed me, saying, "May the Lord use this child to bring about a revival in China."[1] My English first name is Harry and my middle name is Francis. There is no Chinese translation for these two names, but it is remarkable that my Chinese name also captures the beginning sounds of Harry and Francis.

When God appeared to Moses in the flaming bush and called him to go to Egypt, Moses asked God what his name was. "God said to Moses, 'I AM WHO I AM. This is what you are to say to the Israelites: "I AM has sent me to you"'" (Exod 3:14).

The infinite God cannot be contained within a single name. How would the Israelites come to know who the I AM was? They did not have the Bible. It was not written yet. They would, however, get to know a great deal about him through the miracles and wonders he performed. We know this because we now have the

---

1. Winslow, *By Love Compelled*, 78.

Bible which records the many amazing miracles and wonders he performed for the Israelites.

Why did the generation of Israelites after Moses and Joshua not know the Lord? One reason was they did not know "what he had done for Israel" (Judg 2:10b). They had forgotten about his mighty miracles.

Many people in Western countries, where Christianity has a long history, have turned away from faith in God, becoming indifferent to God or rejecting his existence altogether. They are like the generation of Israelites after Moses and Joshua who no longer knew God, who forgot the mighty miracles he had done.

Some may acknowledge God performed miracles in the Bible, but they do not believe he still does miracles today. God's character never changes. The stories in this book testify that he is still the God of miracles and wonders.

I have chosen to use several names of Jesus in the titles of my book. "King of Kings and Lord of Lords" is sung repeatedly in the Hallelujah chorus as the audience stands near the end of the world-famous oratorio Handel's *Messiah*, which has been performed multiple times with large choirs and orchestras in Shanghai and many other cities around the world. This is one of the names of Jesus, for "on his robe and on his thigh he has this name written: KING OF KINGS AND LORD OF LORDS" (Rev 19:16). Four other names of Jesus, which resonate with meaning and blessing, designate the four periods of my life: "And he will be called Wonderful Counselor, Mighty God, Everlasting Father, Prince of Peace" (Isa 9:6b).

This book contains the true stories of many miracles and wonders. *I have put a space before and after each miracle to designate where the story begins and ends.* I hope you will be able to see Jesus more clearly through them. He wants to do miracles and wonders today in your life as well.

"I will remember the deeds of the Lord;
yes, I will remember your miracles of long ago."

(Ps 77:11)

Special credit belongs to my two editors
Julie Winslow and Riley Bonds
who helped make my manuscript
a much better book than it was before.

PART ONE

1938–41

"And he will be called . . . Prince of Peace."

(Isa 9:6b)

"Prince of Peace"—this name of Jesus is an excellent foundation for the beginning of my life. He surrounded my family with
peace in the midst of turmoil and war.

1

Roots

MY FATHER'S NAME WAS Harold Winslow. We can trace his ancestry back to the second voyage of the Mayflower that landed near Plymouth Rock. Dad grew up on a beautiful farm in Brockport, Pennsylvania, with several brothers and sisters, including an identical twin brother, Harry.

I do not know which brother in this picture is Harold. Nobody could tell the twins apart except their mother. When one got sick, the doctor would bring medicine for both as the other twin would invariably get sick, too.

Twins often have some interesting stories and

my dad and uncle were no exceptions. When my mother and dad were to be married, she made him promise that it would be him coming down the church aisle, not Harry. Even she could not tell them apart!

Once, Dad went to a big building some distance from where he lived and saw his brother right there at the entrance. He extended his arm to shake hands, but then it dawned on him that his brother was not there. The solid glass was only reflecting himself.

Another time, Dad went into a barber shop and the confused barber said to him, "I just cut your hair." Dad grinned and replied, "My hair grows fast."

My grandfather was very ill and bedridden with heart trouble, perhaps because he worked too hard when he owned a sawmill in another town. My dad, Harold, encouraged his brother, Harry, to go to college while he stayed home to help his mom care for his dad. Grandpa's weakness lasted more than ten years.

One day during family devotions, they read Job 5:26: "You will come to the grave in full vigor, like sheaves gathered in season." These words really spoke to Grandpa and God gave him faith to believe it for himself. The next morning when Dad went into Grandpa's bedroom, he wasn't there! He had gotten up because he was healed. Soon after, Grandpa went deer hunting with Dad and some friends.

I never met Grandpa, but I did meet Grandma. In my mind's eye, I can still see her, stately and plump, sitting on the farmhouse porch, knitting as she enjoyed the beautiful scenery in front of her. I was very young then, probably four or five years old. I quietly slipped down the sloped yard to see the dolls in the little tent there when no girl cousins were around. Of course, I was scared someone would see me, so I didn't dare linger.

I remember visiting the farm when I was older and having immense fun playing among the hay bales in the barn with my cousin, Dave. I found the farmhouse fascinating. It was three stories tall with a small turret at the top so you could look out and see when the farmers had started back from the fields and know it was time to get supper on the table. There were not one, but two, living rooms and plenty of bedrooms. One of my aunts lived there after Grandma went to heaven. She rented bedrooms to hunters in deer season. There was good hunting in those Pennsylvania hills.

Some years later, I visited Brockport again and met my dad's youngest brother who was living in the valley down below the farmhouse. He told some amazing stories from his experiences in the old days flying small planes to deliver the mail.

My mother, Carolyn, also grew up in a big family. The VanValins had four boys and five girls. Mother is in the first row farthest to the right.

Mother's family lived in Unionville, Pennsylvania, among beautiful countryside. One night when she was very young, several of her siblings were in one of the bedrooms in their house. They looked out the window and saw a bear coming down the street toward their house. They all scrambled under the covers of the big bed and watched the bear out of a hole in the blanket. It kept crawling closer and closer toward their window! They let out a big scream. Then my grandmother yelled out, "Ernest!" She had realized it was one of her older sons who was trying to scare them.

When Mother was a young lady, she became sick with rheumatic fever. Here is the story in her own words:

> Summer came and I went with the family to Mill Hall camp meeting. We took two tents for the eleven of us. I

5

lay on the bed and listened to the singing. After six days, I had such a longing to be in a service that I ventured slowly and cautiously toward the chair at the edge of the Tabernacle. They were about to have a healing service before the preaching.

I am so sick. It would be presumptuous for me to go, I thought. *I should pray and read the Word and find His will.* Others went and knelt at the altar. As I knelt quietly by my chair, I felt an unutterable pull to go, so I did.

When the pastors laid their hands on my head that Thursday, it was as if I had hold of a battery . . . I was still weak, but on Sunday, my brother Ernest helped me go to the service and took a cushion for me. Sister Nellie Haskins, a pastor's wife, motioned for me to sit in front in a chair by her, so Ernest took me.

When they had testimonies, I testified to my obedience in being anointed, and that I was trusting God to guide. As I sat and listened to others, a strong impression came to me. "Carolyn, get up and go to the other end of the altar." I was surprised and perplexed. *What would I do at the other end of the altar?* I asked myself. I began to feel troubled and could not enjoy the testimonies. It came again, "Carolyn, get up and go to the other end of the altar."

Was this of God? If so, I would be willing to do anything, but I feared doing anything in the flesh. Finally, with tears running down my cheeks, I turned to Sister Haskins.

"My child, do what the Lord tells you," she said. I did, and as I went toward the altar, I felt as light as a feather. I began to run, and when I got back to my chair, I just couldn't stop running. . . . God's Spirit was marvelously evident.

I finally felt I should sit down and quietly did so. Others were still praising the Lord. Brother Barkas, the district elder, came to me and said quietly, "Carolyn, I noticed when you sat down you were not out of breath." It dawned on me. I was healed! I knew that if I had run like that before the healing service, I would have dropped dead.[1]

---

1. Winslow, *By Love Compelled*, 32–33. Emphasis original.

One of the most interesting VanValin stories down through the years included high suspense. As a dentist, Grandpa VanValin made sufficient money to support his family well. For years they had lived in a house by the railroad tracks, but they had just moved to a nicer house in the village. Not far away, on the other side of the tracks from their first home, was a prison. Sometimes a convict would escape from the jail. They would hide out nearby until a freight train came through and they could jump on board to escape.

Grandpa's family had not yet moved all of their belongings to the new house, including their family cow. Each evening Grandma called a son to go to the old house and milk the cow. One night, Francis said, "I think I'll just stay there tonight after milking the cow."

Grandma said, "I don't think you should stay overnight. I heard another convict has escaped from the jail."

Francis reassured her, "I'll be all right. Forrest will come with me." Forrest was the youngest son. Off the two boys went.

Forrest milked the cow and put the bucket in the cold milk room, which was part of the house. After locking the front door, the boys went to the bedroom at the end of the hallway and tried to settle down to sleep. It was easy to wonder if this was such a good thing after all, thinking about the escaped convict in the area, but Francis was not afraid.

Suddenly, they heard the milk room window go up, then a splash! Francis knew he had left the milk bucket under the window, so someone must have stepped into it after climbing through the window. Someone was breaking into their house!

Francis quietly got out of bed, crept over to the drawer, got out the pistol, and gave it to Forrest, who was cowering under the blanket. Francis grabbed the big metal alarm clock from the stand and hid with it behind the open door of their bedroom. He was going to hit the intruder's head with it if he came into their room.

They listened intently as the person moved through the house. The intruder slowly walked down the hallway, searching the bedrooms on either side. They assumed he was gathering loot and making sure no one was there. Closer and closer he came. Then he was standing right at their doorway, but he didn't come in. He turned and walked back down the hallway to the master bedroom, where their parents had slept. He went in and sat on the bed. Plop! One shoe came off, then the other. He apparently wanted to get some sleep before the freight train came by.

Then the man let out a long sigh and the boys immediately knew it was their father! They had recognized the sound of his usual sigh as he lay down on the bed after a long day's work. Whew, what a relief!

Later, the whole story was recounted to the rest of the family. After working at the dental clinic, Grandpa had gone home to their new house and Grandma had told him that their two sons were staying overnight at the old house. He had come over to make sure they were all right. When he found the front door locked, he decided to let himself in through the milk room window, but in the dark he didn't know the milk bucket was there. He had searched bedrooms coming down the hallway, looking for which room the boys were in. Coming finally to the bedroom at the end of the hallway, he could see that the bed was occupied so he didn't go in. He didn't want to wake them up. "I wish I had run down the hallway into your boys' room," Grandpa said.

To this Francis solemnly replied, "I'm glad you didn't. I could have killed you with that alarm clock."

Mother received her college education at Greenville College in Greenville, Illinois. By the time she finished her senior year, she had completed three majors—history, English literature, and secondary education—and two minors—science and languages! After graduation, she taught at Spring Arbor Junior College in Spring Arbor, Michigan.

Dad came from the farm in Pennsylvania to enter Greenville College. Because he had waited until his father's health improved, he was several years older than most of his classmates. After graduating, he attended biblical Seminary in New York.

Dad and Mother had met each other previously in a camp meeting in Pennsylvania, before he came as a student to Greenville, but it was during this time at different schools that they began writing to each other. Mother numbered the letters that came— there were 386. They had fallen in love!

After Dad finished his seminary studies, my parents were married in Spring Arbor on August 16, 1932. They first lived in Greenville, Illinois, where Dad had become a professor at Greenville College. Their first child, Paul, was born there.

My parents sensed that God had clearly called them to become missionaries. They applied to the FM General Missionary Board, which appointed them to China. They left for China by ship, the *Hikawa Maru*, in September 1936.

2

In the Shadow of the Almighty

ARMIES OF THE NATIONALISTS and Communists had been fighting for power in various regions of China for nearly ten years when my parents arrived in 1936. An intrepid band of missionaries welcomed them to Kaifeng in Henan Province, the center of our Free Methodist Church's work in China. My parents stand third and fourth from the left in this picture. I have met three others in this picture: on the far left, Nurse Pearl Reid, and on the far right, Alice and James Hudson Taylor II, whose famous grandfather James Hudson Taylor founded the China Inland Mission.

In the southern part of Henan Province lies a village called Ji Gong Shan (Rooster Mountain). Its name reflects its location—the mountain peak under which it nestles resembles a male chicken's head.

Missionaries in that region of China often spent summers there to escape the heat of the lower plains.

When the Sino-Japanese War began to spread its damage across the country in 1937, my parents and young Paul retreated to Ji Gong Shan to await my arrival. Mother was afraid she would not have anyone with medical training to help with my birth since it was offseason and many visiting missionaries had returned to the plains. God knew this need. When it came time to give birth, a medical doctor and two nurses were present to help her. I came into the world just fine on March 31, 1938.

Holding Han Fu: Dr. Mary Taylor from England; left, Nurse Danielson from Norway; right, Nurse Hunt from Australia.

While Dad was away attending our church's annual conference, Mother stayed alone with Paul and me in our rented house, Number 23, at Ji Gong Shan. She prayed often for safety and wisdom, knowing that the war and bandits presented real dangers to herself and her traveling husband.

One night, Mother was awakened by a quick, sharp thud and leapt out of bed thinking bandits were trying to break into the house. She looked closely at one of the widows and realized it had been a large Chinese beetle that had made the loud noise. In her nervousness, when she tried to smash the bug, she pressed her hand so hard against the window that the glass broke. Thankfully, she didn't injure her hand.

As she lay there trying to go back to sleep, she heard a voice in the darkness—"Sweetheart!" She leapt back out of bed to greet Harold, who had been absent longer than expected. After their joy and relief at being reunited subsided, Harold explained what had transpired.

After the conference had ended, he had gone to gather warmer bedding since they had not originally planned to stay in the cold mountains so long. When he tried to get on the train to return, so many refugees were swarming around that he could not get even to the steps of the train. He threw his roll of bedding inside an open window and crawled in after it. Halfway home, they heard Japanese bombers overhead. The engineer disconnected the engine and ran it down the tracks while the passengers scattered and lay down in the nearby rice fields for over two hours hiding from the enemy. Instead of bombing the train or tracks, the enemy bombed a train station down the way. After the coast was clear, the engineer brought his engine back, reconnected it to the train, and they continued cautiously on their way.

When Harold finally got off the train near Ji Gong Shan, he walked through dangerous territory where bandits had been five miles in the dark to finally arrive at their mountain home. What a miracle of God's protection!

> *Whoever dwells in the shelter of the Most High will rest in the shadow of the Almighty. I will say of the LORD, "He is my refuge and my fortress, my God, in whom I trust." Surely he will save you from the fowler's snare and from the deadly pestilence. He will cover you with his feathers, and*

under his wings you will find refuge; his faithfulness will
be your shield and rampart. You will not fear the terror of
night, nor the arrow that flies by day. (Ps 91:1–5)

Shortly after this, our little family of four began the arduous journey to our newly appointed mission station in Qixian in the northern plains of Henan. We traveled by train, ambulance, and an oxcart pulled by three cows and a donkey before facing the mighty Yellow River. The dikes and bridges had been destroyed by the Chinese to hinder the advance of the Japanese army, so water had flooded nearby farmland and farmers had turned into ferrymen to transport supplies and refugees across the widened river. We piled on a small boat, and my mother set me in my bamboo-basket bed down on the deck next to her. Suddenly, another passenger gasped and they all turned just in time to see a large, overhanging tree limb narrowly sweep past my basket. Instead, it caught two boat-men by surprise and they had to scramble quickly to avoid being tossed into the swift, muddy waters! Once again, our family was covered by the wings of the Almighty.

We finally made it to Qixian in the north plains of Henan, which was an important location for our work. The Sino-Japanese War was still raging on. The Japanese army surrounded our city and were shooting above the city walls.

One day a bullet came crashing through my nursery room. Thankfully, at that moment I was downstairs in the living room with my family where we were having family devotions. Dad was reading Ps 91, reminding us that our refuge was in our Heavenly Father's hands. The bullet hit a nail in the wall near my bed and ricocheted through the floor to the first level where it finally bur-rowed under a rug.

Dad told Mother to always keep the front door locked be-cause Japanese soldiers might show up at any moment. Dad was out helping the many refugees who had crowded into the church compound when Japanese soldiers burst into the city. When the soldiers arrived at our house, one of them began to beat violently on the front door. Mother grabbed a United States flag and threw it over her shoulder. Then holding me, her infant son, in her other arm, she opened the door. The soldier burst through the door and thrust his bayonet at my mother's face, but thankfully did not shove it any further. After a short while they left.

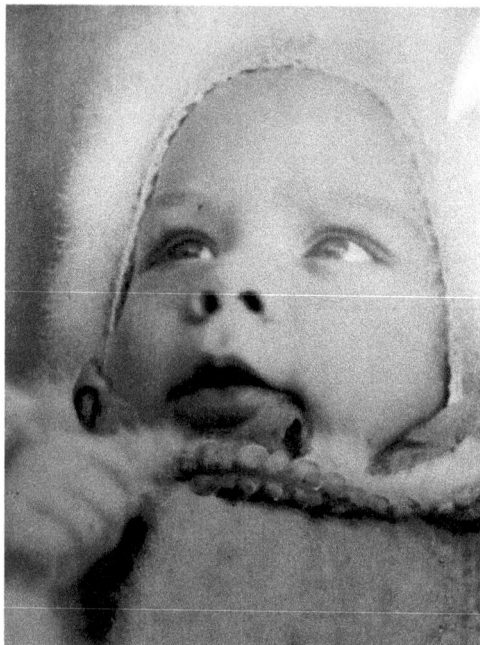

Another day, Mother was home alone and discovered a Chinese soldier trying to pose as our cook in the kitchen with an apron on. She told him to leave, but he refused. Just then Japanese soldiers came to our house and began searching it. If they had found that Chinese soldier in our kitchen, we could have been in big trouble, but they never went into the kitchen. Why didn't they find him?

In those days, we didn't have an electric washing machine or dryer. We washed by hand and hung our clothes to dry on a large, multitiered wooden rack. The rack stood right in front of the kitchen door with my diapers hanging all over it, blocking it from the view of the soldiers. After they left, Mother opened the door and found an empty kitchen. The Chinese soldier had run away.

Dad's work in the church helping refugees was also risky business. A Japanese soldier once drew his sword against Dad in anger. Praise God, he did not use it further. Still another time, a Japanese

14

soldier came up to Dad and said in a quiet voice, "Amen." Dad realized he must be a Christian and replied, "Hallelujah." These two words sound very similar in many languages. How amazing that an American missionary and a Japanese soldier would meet each other in China, brothers in Christ!

Another time, Dad was at home when the Japanese soldiers came to search our house. They searched all the way up to the attic. When a door was opened, lo and behold, another Chinese soldier was hiding there! Dad quickly explained to the Japanese soldiers how the man could have gotten in without his knowledge. He wanted to make sure they knew he wasn't purposely harboring their enemies. As he was describing all this, the Chinese soldier escaped.

I was about two years old in this picture, wearing padded clothes handed down from my brother, Paul. Although they were bulky, they really helped keep me warm in the winter.

When I was two and a half, Dad became very ill from a mysterious disease. The doctors couldn't identify it, but they told him he would die in China if we did not go home to America. Soon, our family left on a large passenger ship for the long journey. Mother told what happened in the middle of the voyage:

> It was a three-week journey across the ocean. Harold sat up for meals four times on that voyage. We were designated to sit at the captain's table. One night, the captain was not there. Our ship began to heave, rise, and fall. All at once there was a great lurch, and away Paul and I went as well as our plates of food. I slid between other tables

and right through the serving of mashed potatoes and gravy and the rest.

Stewards, in their white coats, hastened to pick Paul up—far from me. When they tried to pick me up, I began to laugh until I was a dead weight. A spectacle I was! I looked back, and little Harry in his high chair was the only one at the table. He was crying his heart out.[1]

God's protection was evident and we eventually arrived safely in San Francisco.

1. Winslow, *By Love Compelled*, 110–11.

PART TWO

1941–60

"And he will be called ... Everlasting Father."

(ISA 9:6B)

THIS NAME FOR JESUS, "Everlasting Father," holds significant meaning for the second period of my journey. He is my Everlasting Father—then, now, and forever.

3

In His Care

WHEN WE RETURNED FROM China, we went to Williamsport, Pennsylvania, to visit Uncle Francis, Uncle Forrest, and their families. My very first memory happened there. I remember looking down the street and was simply amazed by the big trees on either side of the road. I must not have seen anything like that in China.

Soon we settled in Winona Lake, Indiana, where we bought a house. We lived close to the beautiful lake, which we could see from the house when the leaves were not on the trees. I learned to swim in Winona Lake. Paul and I had lots of fun playing hide-and-seek with other children—swinging around the pillars holding up the end of the long pier, diving off the low diving board, jumping off the high diving board, and swimming to and from the raft that was anchored nearby.

Dad's illness got better, and he was chosen to be general missionary board secretary of our Free Methodist Church in 1942. This was the top administrative position over world missions of our denomination. Before long, his illness came back worse than before and he was not able to continue working, so he resigned in 1944. He visited the Mayo Clinic and finally discovered that his illness was tuberculosis. By that time, it had already spread to his spine. They operated, taking a bone from his leg and placing it by his spine, but it was too late. God took him home to heaven when I was only six years old. I was too young to comprehend everything, but I knew Mother was very, very sad.

My fondest memory of Dad was during our family devotions. He read to us from Herbert's *Story of the Bible*, which had beautiful pictures that captured the attention of little boys. Paul sat on a little chair next to Dad. I got the best spot, right on his lap.

In the winters, Paul and I had great fun sledding down steep Evangel Hill Road, not far from where were we lived in Winona Lake. Evangel Hill got its name from the Billy Sunday Tabernacle, nearby in the park. The hill and the park were connected by a small path. A street ran along the bottom of the hill, and usually a policeman stood there to stop cars when people were sledding down the hill. Paul would lay down first on the sled, and then I would push with all my might before jumping on top of him. We were one of the fastest sleds for our young age group of seven- to ten-year-olds. If the conditions were just right, we could keep going at the bottom of the hill for one or two more blocks, which was almost to the canal.

One time I decided to try sledding on my own. I jumped on and went flying down the hill, but suddenly realized there wasn't a policeman at the bottom. I saw a car coming, but I hadn't learned how to stop yet, so the sled kept right on going. The car stopped just as I plowed into it. Cars back then often had a runner along the bottom of the door to step on. I had hit the runner, which prevented me from going under the car. That experience shook me up, but I didn't have any real injuries. After that I learned how to control the sled.

One of our favorite things to do was to interlock a bunch of sleds together in a long line. To do this, each rider would lay face down and hook their boots in the front two holes of the sled behind them. The rider on the front sled would zigzag down the hill weaving like a snake and making the line behind him do the same. This gave the rider on the last sled a really wild ride!

Paul and I had fun at home also. We built model airplanes out of construction sets. These were not like the sets for kids today with hard plastic pieces. Ours had balsa wood pieces, so the construction was closer to the way real planes are made. We would put a thick rubber band in the fuselage and attach it to the propeller so that it would fly just a bit after the propeller was wound tight. We glued colored paper onto the balsa wood wings and fuselage, added symbols, and presto—there was our completed fighter plane to hang from the ceiling above our beds. Paul hung his planes above his bed and I hung mine above my bed. What a beautiful sight for two little boys!

Paul was bigger and older than me, so he could easily catch me if I ran in a straight line. When we were in the house, sometimes I would tease him and run to the dining room where I would run around the table and he could not catch me. It was my safe spot.

One time I started teasing Paul while I was standing at the doorway to our bedroom and he was at the other end of the room with his friend, a boy who lived up the hill near us. I knew I could get to the dining room table in time. I was not expecting what happened next.

The other boy was holding a flashlight in his hand and he suddenly threw it at me. It flew clear across the room and hit me right in the face, breaking off half of one of my top incisor teeth. Of course, I bawled like a stuck pig!

The dentist pulled the remaining stump of my tooth and then made me a plate with a false tooth on the end to fill in the gap in my teeth. I was only a kid, not an eighty-year-old man, so I had some fun with the situation. When I was sitting in church and a little child was eyeing me over their parent's shoulder and Mother wasn't looking, I would drop the plate down in my mouth and wiggle the tooth around to scare the child.

Every few years as my mouth grew larger, I got a new plate. This process finally ended just before Ruth and I took our first trip to Hong Kong when a renowned Christian dentist implanted a permanent tooth. I've had it for decades without any problem at all.

When I was fifteen, Mother was sent as a missionary to Taiwan. She was the second missionary of our denomination to arrive there; Geneva Sayer (chapter 17) was the first. Mother, Paul, and I left from the West Coast and sailed on a Maersk freighter across the Pacific to Taiwan. One early morning in the middle of the ocean, the alarm rang: *Fire, fire!* We immediately went out on deck and saw flames shooting up, coming out of the freighter's engine room.

Mom quickly went back and put on her best dress, not knowing how long we might be in lifeboats. Without an engine for propulsion, we were dead in the water, a very bad situation indeed. After some time passed, the sailors managed to put out the fire, and we were able to continue our journey. Thank God this did not happen in rough seas!

I attended Morrison Academy, a small Christian boarding school for missionary children in Taichung. I entered as a sophomore during the second year of the school's existence. At the time, it consisted of a two-story school building and several houses that functioned as dormitories. One night, something very unusual happened.

We high school boys slept in bunk beds in a room at the end of the dormitory. I was sleeping in the bottom bunk, in the bed farthest away from the two doors to the room. All of a sudden, I awoke and looked through my mosquito net to the other end of the room. In the dark, I saw the form of a man moving slowly beside a desk. By the way he moved, I knew it was not a student. I had raised my head to look, so I laid my head back down quietly and tried to think of what to do. The bathroom was very close to where he was, so it would be easy for him to run out the bathroom door to the courtyard and escape. If I tried to get out of bed, he would hear me open my mosquito net and run.

Suddenly in the dark it appeared the intruder was crouching right beside my bed trying to see if I was asleep. I let out a big scream! He raced out of the dorm. All the boys in our room woke up. Running out to the courtyard, we discovered several things the man had tried to steal, but he ran away so fast he hadn't picked them up. We could see the spot where he had come and gone over the wall where the sharp shards of glass on top had been broken flat.

The wonder of it was, first, that none of us had been harmed by this robber, and second, when we returned to our room, we discovered he had not found the tuition money one boy had stashed in a small drawer even though the robber had opened other drawers right next to it. One top-bunk boy put a long mountain tribal knife under his pillow and warned us: "No one get up in the night." We did not!

TENTH AND ELEVENTH GRADES

I was captain of our basketball team, the Morrison Mustangs. In 1955, we played games against Chinese soldiers, civilians, a United States Army team, and our faculty. We usually won that first year, but the 1956 season games were tougher.

I enjoyed an interesting three years of high school, graduating third in my class. There were only three of us. The picture on the left above was taken our junior year. We were the first graduating class of Morrison Academy. Ted Chandler is standing on the left in the back. I am beside him, and Phil Bly is in front of me.

Even though the school was small, we kept busy with lots of activities besides our academic studies. Beside my senior picture in the yearbook was the following caption which shows my favorite verse and what year of high school I attended these activities: "Eph. 3:16–21, Activities: CYA Pres. 3, Orchestra 2, 3, 4, *The Morrison* 4, Sports 3, 4, Echo 2, 3."[1]

Mother lived a four-hour drive south of me in Pingtung when I studied at Morrison Academy. During holidays and summer months, I would go home to stay with her. I remember well what happened one day when I was there. Two men came up to our front gate. One was carrying the other on his back. He asked Mother for money to help his friend, who supposedly could not walk. Mother told him to talk to our Chinese pastor since we were living right beside the church. As his argument did not prevail with Mother, the man on his back slid down and the two of them walked away. It was a sham.

Mother loved children. She started a class for them in her home where she told them Bible stories. Her class was well attended until one day when the children suddenly stopped coming. She couldn't figure out what had happened. Then she found out a monk from the nearby temple had warned the children not to go to our house, saying, "The foreign woman will eat you!"

In hindsight, Mother should not have held the class in her house. In fact, we should not have been living in a house within the church compound because people who were not Christian could easily think that Christianity was a foreigner's religion and then not want to come to the church. But Mother did not have the opportunity to take cross-culture studies like I had the privilege to take later.

The summer after graduating from Morrison Academy, I took my first airplane ride. I traveled by myself from Taiwan to the United States in a double-decked Flying Clipper airplane. I was so tired from travel and jet lag when I got to my uncle's home on the West Coast that I slept through the night and almost through the

1. Pictures in this section are from the 1955 and 1956 *Morrisonian* yearbooks.

whole next day before getting up. People kept coming to check on me to see if I was still alive.

Once I recovered from my travels, I came by bus from California all the way to Illinois to attend Greenville College. When I arrived at the bus station in the town of Greenville, I had to ask someone how to get to the college. I knew no one there. That soon changed and I made many good friends.

I had a good freshman year. President Long was kind to me and let me stay in the dorm during vacations when students usually went home since my mother was still living in Taiwan. I was able to buy a Ford Sedan from Professor Tidball and that summer I decided to drive west to where my brother Paul was working in California.

When I got to California, Paul was working at a railroad tunnel that was being built through a mountain in California. He drove a big, front-dump truck. The bed of the truck was in front of him as he drove it into the tunnel and then the big machine that excavated the rock and dirt would continually throw it into the bed. When it was full, he would back out of the tunnel because it was too narrow to turn around in. After backing out, Paul would turn around, drive to the dump site, gun the motor to go faster, and then slam on the brakes so the front bed would tip forward to spill its contents. There was no automatic off-load.

One of the front-dumping truck operators left the job so I went with Paul to the site and applied. I got the job. I had never driven a diesel truck before, much less a front-dumper, but I was a fast learner and Paul showed me how it was done. I got my own truck and began. Things went well until the second or third day. I got too close to one side of the tunnel and scraped along the large air duct. I stopped, and the foreman had to come and drive it out. That was scary, and I drove extra carefully after that.

The man who had left returned and got his driving job back, so I was out of work. My next job was in a large fruit canning factory. My task, with another guy whose morals were much different than mine, was to paste large labels on gallon cans of fruit cocktail.

When that job ended, I drove into the mountains of California looking for more work.

I found work on a site that was blasting large rocks in a shallow tunnel that was being prepared to lay pipe. My job was to stand and manipulate by hand a jack hammer to drive holes in the rocks for laying dynamite. I had to push down hard for the bit to penetrate the rock. If the bit broke, there could be a terrible accident. It was a good-paying job, and God helped me not get hurt.

When all the holes had been drilled, I helped a welder who was welding pipes together in the shallow tunnel. I was his go-fer, getting things he needed for the welding. He was not a very nice man, and I then found another job preparing the tall banks on the side of the road that was being built in the mountains.

During my mountain work in California, I slept outside in my little pup tent. I would drive to a spot near the lake where no one was around, pitch the tent, and cook my evening meal in a can. While it was still light, I would walk down a small trail to the lake and take a bath.

One day, after bathing, I got back to my locked car and found I did not have the key. Without the key, I had no way to get in or drive the car. How was I going to get to work the next day? I had to find that key!

I knew God knew where it was. I earnestly prayed that he would help me find it. I walked back down the trail looking for it all the way to the lake, but I didn't find it. I came back up the trail all the way to the car, but I still didn't find it. My anxiety was rapidly mounting. God knew right where that key was. Why wasn't he helping me find it?

I retraced my walk to the lake and back a second time, but I still couldn't find the key. It was getting dark. I could only walk to the lake one more time. The third time when I got to the lake, I had a new thought. Why not look in the water? I went over to where I had sat earlier by the shore and when I put my hand down in the water, I immediately felt the key on the bottom. God answered my prayer! It was an important lesson God wanted me to learn. I was in his care and could leave the timing for the answer up to him.

It was high time to get back to Greenville College. Classes had already begun and I still had to drive back to Illinois. It was worth the delay, though, since I had made very good money.

Mother and Paul were able to visit me at Greenville when she was on furlough from Taiwan. I am standing on the left of the picture, and Paul is on the right.

4

My Beloved

When I arrived back to Greenville, I was already two weeks late for school. Some very important things had happened during those weeks that I knew nothing about. I went to the dining hall and, standing in the cafeteria line, I looked across the room and saw a gorgeously beautiful girl I had never seen before. Our eyes met!

I soon learned her name was Ruth, and she was the daughter of missionaries to China and India. Not only that, during the first meeting of the Missions Club while I was away, she had been elected secretary. I had been chosen president of the club the year before, so she was now my secretary. Wow! This was not a coincidence!

We had assigned seating in chapel, so she sat one row in front of me, a few seats to the left. I could gaze at her without anyone knowing.

We would glance at each other when studying in the library. When I finally had the nerve to ask her for a date, she refused and I was crushed. Later, I learned the reason. Another young man was pursuing her.

On her way from her home in India to the United States to go to college, Ruth had traveled across the Pacific in a ship with a missionary lady. This lady kept telling her about her son who was in the United States military. When they got to the West Coast, her son drove Ruth and his mother across half the country to drop her off at Greenville. He was smitten with Ruth and it was obvious he wanted to keep seeing her.

Ruth felt she needed to make a clean break with him before going out with me. I waited in the wings. Finally, she was free to say yes to me for our first date. Just before we went on that date, one of my good friends in the men's dorm told me he felt God wanted him to ask Ruth for a date. I happily told him that Ruth and I had already planned to have a date. God's timing was perfect. That was the first of many dates. Ruth, with her British-educated background, kept a journal of our dates and even made a scrapbook about them.

Ruth had spent her teenage years in India and graduated from a very strict British high school which offered an extra year of classes. During grade 13, students studied hard to take the Cambridge Exam. As a result, Greenville College gave Ruth a full year of college credit for passing the Cambridge Exam. Thus, she came in as a sophomore, which was my sophomore year as well.

Ruth felt God wanted her to be a nurse, and she hoped to return to India as a missionary nurse. She wanted to go to nursing school after her sophomore year at Greenville. I was thinking of taking graduate studies at Asbury Theological Seminary in Wilmore, Kentucky, so she found a nursing program at Good Samaritan Hospital in Lexington. It would take three years to obtain her RN degree. I knew that I had two more years at Greenville, but we could be near each other during her last year of nursing school when I began my studies at the seminary.

Absence makes the heart grow fonder. I tried to make the long, round-trip drive from Greenville to Lexington once a month. I missed her greatly and was so very glad when I could see her.

Then something totally unexpected happened. The army man who had first driven Ruth to Greenville with his mother came all the way from California to Lexington to see her again. He made it plain that he would continue to pursue her unless she was engaged to another. Enough of this! Ruth and I had already been dating about two years. We got engaged right away.

During my time at Greenville, I had the opportunity to work for a few months driving a big semitruck. We mainly carried Illinois-grown soybeans to the grain elevators next to the Mississippi River by St. Louis. During soybean harvest, a fleet of trucks busily ran back and forth to that spot. A full semitruck carried a heavy load.

One day, I fully loaded my truck and was driving it on a two-lane road that had a curved upward lip on the shoulder of the cement pavement. It would have been dangerous if I drove up onto the shoulder. I was almost to a bend in the road when another semitruck came blasting around the bend from the opposite direction. He was cutting into my lane trying to make better time. There was no way I could stop. Seeing me, he tried to compensate, but he was too close. Bang! My outside mirror exploded right next to my driver's seat. If the truck had been a few inches closer, that might have been the end of me. How amazing! It was God's grace.

At the end of my junior year, I was tired of driving the long trip between Greenville and Lexington to see Ruth, so I decided to apply to study at Asbury College in Wilmore, Kentucky. I was going to be a college senior, and I still planned to graduate from Greenville College. I had been assured as my first three college years were here I could take my senior year at another college and still graduate here.

I was accepted at Asbury College to continue my history major and was delighted to be close to Ruth. The first few weeks of school went smoothly, but I didn't know how strict the Asbury College president could be about following administrative rules.

I wanted to earn some money at a part-time job in Lexington. In order to do that, I had to ask permission from the college president since it was a job outside of the school. I went to see him. To my astonishment, he became angry at me. When he heard about my situation, he told me I had to leave the college. "We do not accept transfer seniors!" Once he learned that I planned to graduate from Greenville instead of Asbury, that was the last straw. I absolutely had to leave!

I tried reasoning with him. I had been accepted by Asbury College Admissions and was already attending classes. I offered him a compromise. Could I stay if I agreed to graduate from Asbury instead of Greenville? He finally relented and let me stay. I did have to take extra summer courses since their requirements for the history major were different from Greenville's, but it was worth it and I gained more experience by attending two different Christian colleges.

While at Asbury College, I attended their ministerial club. The student president of the club that year had a lot of talent. I looked up to him and thought it would be great if he became a missionary because he was so gifted. In my naivety, I prayed and thought I would talk to him about this if he showed up at a certain building on campus when I was there. I had not talked to him about meeting me there. Well, do you think he came? He did not.

Before the school year ended, the ministerial club men decided they would take a three-day retreat like the year before. We would fast and pray that the Holy Spirit would come like he had the previous year. We would only eat one small meal of mostly bread and water each day. A faculty member joined us the first night. After that we were on our own.

We prayed and prayed for the Holy Spirit to come, but nothing happened. I distinctly remember when the leader of one session berated another person who was there. I felt this was wrong. The tone of voice and words used against him were not good.

On the last day, we were directed to go out by ourselves to different places around the camp and pray. I wanted to get farther away, so I made my way past a building at the edge of camp. As I came around the corner, I saw something strange in the middle of a tree about fifteen yards away from me. There were no other trees between me and that tree, only an open field. I could see a white glow in the tree, but I couldn't make out the form completely. It was not demonic; it was pure and good. It was an angel, and it was looking straight at me.

I also sensed it was not pleased with me. I did not feel a condoning presence, but rather a reprimand. I could clearly sense its displeasure. It was showing me I was wrong. I felt a great sense of awe, but was frightened at the same time. Without drawing any nearer, I gradually backed away around the corner, then continued walking slowly all the way to my bed and lay down.

I did not understand immediately, but later it became clear why the angel had appeared to me. We had been very earnest in praying for the Holy Spirit to move, but it was so we could receive an experience and go back and brag to our classmates about what had happened. Our desire was not for the Holy Spirit to fill us so he could use us to bless and help others. To further complicate things, there had not been harmony in the camp. Our motives were wrong. We should have been seeking him in humility, not an experience to boast about in pride.

5

Happiest By a Lot

AFTER I GRADU-
ATED FROM Asbury
College in 1960,
Ruth and I married
on September 5.
We had a few un-
usual twists to our
wedding story.

Ruth still had
one more year of
nursing school at
Good Samaritan
Hospital. She only had five days of vacation from school and we
were getting married in northern Ontario, her childhood home.
Driving to Ontario and back was an 1,800-mile drive, and she had
to be back to the hospital by 7:00 a.m. on the sixth day!

We had a lovely wedding service. Ruth's parents, William and
Evangeline Smith, and much of her extended family were present.
My mother was still a missionary in Taiwan, so she could not at-
tend, but we had her blessing.

Ruth tells more about it in her autobiography: "The wedding itself was simple, but elegant. My father walked me up the aisle, gave me away, led the wedding vows, and even served as the photographer. My mother's sisters provided the flowers and cake, and the extended Warren clan helped with lots of other arrangements that day."[1]

Following the wedding, we all went out to have a wonderful meal at a local restaurant. Ruth and I soon after had to dash back to Lexington. No time for a honeymoon. That could come later. We had a tight deadline.

After a long drive, we arrived at the Canada–United States border. We were not prepared for what happened next. Since Ruth was a Canadian citizen, the United States customs officer refused to let her enter the United States! There were people who weren't really married but claimed to be just to get their partner across the border. But this was not us! I argued with the official for some time about us having just gotten married and explained how Ruth had to get back to her nursing school in Kentucky, but it was to no avail. Ruth was outside in the car crying.

Finally, we thought of a plan. I asked the customs officer to call the hospital in Lexington to verify that Ruth was truly a student nurse there. I gave him the phone number and, thankfully, he was willing to call. Yes, it was the truth! He let us go and we made it back in time for Ruth to get to the hospital on time.

We were as poor as church mice that first year, but we did not care. To be together and married was so wonderful. I enrolled at Asbury Theological Seminary (ATS) in the fall. We lived in a little upstairs apartment which fit our needs perfectly since we were both very busy with our schooling. I also worked part time at the local IGA for one dollar an hour. That year we ate a lot of outdated angel food cake.

The second year was easier since Ruth had graduated from nursing school and was offered a full-time job at Good Samaritan Hospital in the busy emergency room. She continued in that job until I graduated from ATS.

1. Winslow, *Love Found a Way*, 69.

My family has often heard me quote this little poem I created to express my love for Ruth, inspired by the poet James Whitcomb Riley:

> When the frost is on the pumpkin and the fodders in the shock,
> And you are my sweetie pumpkins,
> I am the happiest by a lot.

For part of the time I was a student at ATS, I had a job driving a truck that carried asphalt. As I drove the truck, I admired the horse farms with their trim, rolling grasslands and white fences. One day, I dumped my asphalt at the paving machine and started my trip back. A section of the road had already been oiled in preparation for asphalt laying. I knew it was slippery so I drove slowly.

Coming to a ninety-degree turn to the right, I turned the wheel, but the truck did not go to the right—it went straight forward! One of those beautiful white fences was right there in front of me. The truck began to slide in a circle. It had completed 180 degrees when it hit something and stopped. I got out to check the back of the truck. It had hit a low-hanging tree branch. The only thing broken on the truck was a leather strap that held the tailgate. The truck had not hit the beautiful white fence at all. Thank God.

When I first joined this asphalt truck crew, the owner gave me the worst truck. That was his policy. The newest driver got the worst truck. For the most part this truck ran OK, but there was a big problem with the brake fluid—it leaked. Every day before I drove the truck, I had to check the brake fluid, and I also carried an extra can of it in the truck in case it was needed. The brakes seemed to work OK, but it certainly was a nuisance.

One day, I was driving fully loaded through a town on a big four-lane road with a metal divider down the middle. Cars were parked along my right side of the road. I was approaching a traffic light, and cars were stopped ahead of me in both lanes waiting for the light to turn. I stepped on my brake, but nothing happened. The truck just kept going forward. The brake was not working at all! I quickly pulled on the emergency brake which slowed it down, but it was still moving forward. How was I going to keep from smashing into the cars stopped at the traffic light?

Just in time, the light changed, the cars drove on, and I slid through the intersection. That was too close! But I was still moving forward and couldn't stop. The truck finally slowed down enough that I decided to go up a little incline into a gas station to stop. I wasn't sure it would work, but the truck finally came to a halt. Praise God!

Later I was able to get a better truck to drive.

One day when I was driving the newer asphalt truck the rear axle broke. I pulled to the side of the road and waited for the shop mechanic to come and pull the axle out. He discovered that the end cog of the axle had broken off. He looked on the side of the road for the cog but couldn't find it. He finally put a new axle in and said I could drive the truck back home. When I got to the shop the owner, driving another asphalt truck, arrived.

He told me, "I'm sure that cog is still in the differential. I've been driving fast to try and catch you." The mechanic pulled the axle back out. Sure enough, the cog was still in there, lying at the bottom of the differential. If I had hit a big bump, the cog could have torn up the whole differential! The owner remarked, "You must be living right." I knew why I had been protected. My Heavenly Father was watching over me.

PART THREE

1960–83

"And he will be called Wonderful Counselor."

(Isa 9:6b)

THIS NAME FOR JESUS, Wonderful Counselor, represents the third period of my journey. He is my Wonderful Counselor and has faithfully led me through many situations where I needed protection and direction.

6

Surprise and Shock

RUTH SPENT HER EARLY life growing up in China and India. I was in Taiwan three of my teenage years. As missionary kids, we naturally thought about the possibility of missionary service as our own life vocation, and God increasingly made it clear that was what he wanted us to do.

Ruth wanted to go to India as a nurse. I wanted to go to Hong Kong and work among the Chinese. At the time, we were still in college. Nepal had just opened up to missionaries because a Christian doctor in a tourist group had helped heal the Nepali king who had been very sick. For a while, we thought that going to Nepal might be a good compromise. After all, it was situated right between China and India. Later it would become necessary to completely surrender ourselves to wherever God wanted us to go. It had to be left in his hands.

In 1962, I wrote in my journal important lessons I learned about consecration.

> I think that it can be harmful when we hear too many stories of people who have sought and wrestled over sanctification for a period of time, went through all kinds of turmoil as they sought after it, and finally emerged victorious. These kinds of stories are overemphasized

and seem to be almost the norm, as if it is the "real" way to come into the experience. We need not wrestle and strain every effort and go through a great turmoil to accept this experience. We can do it through a single act of complete surrender and faith that God does the work instantaneously, right this very moment, without any delay, if we only would.

In the new birth we consecrate ourselves to do God's will and to be his. Our consecration in entire sanctification is more complete when we are focused on service. We consecrate ourselves totally to be used by him in any way he chooses and give our lives completely for him. In sanctification, we are consecrating our Christian lives more completely to him than when we believe in him in new birth when all there was to consecrate was our lives from sin to God.[1]

During my last year at ATS, Ruth and I went to Winona Lake, Indiana, where we interviewed to become missionaries with the mission board of our denomination. By that time, we both felt led to go as career missionaries to Hong Kong. We soon realized the mission board would be the ones to decide where we would go. A missionary to India said they needed us in India. Another missionary to the Philippines said they needed us in the Philippines.

To complicate things, the mission board had recently appointed one of my best friends from ATS to go to Hong Kong, although they hadn't embarked yet. He had graduated one year before me. When he moved away from Wilmore, I helped him drive a U-Haul truck with his furniture to his new home. We had plenty of time to talk, and I told him all about Hong Kong and China. I had no idea at the time that he and his wife would apply and get appointed to Hong Kong.

Given the needs around the world, we realized it was very unlikely the mission board would appoint two couples to go to Hong Kong at the same time. It seemed hopeless that we would be sent to Hong Kong, and yet that was the place, deep in our hearts, that we wanted to go to work among the Chinese. Were Ruth and I

1. Journal entry, April 1962.

to give up all of our background and knowledge and love of living among them as children?

I will never forget one night during those meetings with the mission board when I knelt beside our bed. I had never prayed such a passionate, agonizing, soul-searing prayer before. I put the decision where we would be sent totally in the Lord's hands. It was up to him, not me.

In my journal, I recorded my surrender: "Made it a matter of prayer and felt definitely that God would direct the mission board so that their decision would be his will for us. It was a time of deeper consecration, for I felt the longing and burden for the Chinese people, yet knew the will of God was best."[2]

There had been one little shaft of light. The mission board secretary, Dr. Byron Lamson, had asked me in the hallway one day where I wanted to go. I immediately answered, "Hong Kong." Before we left, we were told we would need to wait about two weeks before receiving the decision letter.

We waited with great suspense and finally the letter arrived. Upon opening it, we learned that the other couple had been appointed to Africa instead and we were appointed to Hong Kong. What a miracle of God's grace!

> Praise God from whom all blessings flow. Ruth and I cannot properly express the joy and gratitude to God for what he has brought. Truly, this is from the hand of God. It is our call!
>
> We were overwhelmed with praise and joy. How great is our God! It seems like a miracle to us. God has guided.
>
> What a wonderful experience it was to associate with the missionaries, board members, office staff, and candidates at the board meeting. An exceeding privilege it is to be counted now one of their number.[3]

Even after we were appointed, we knew we had to rely on God for the strength to move forward into what he had called us

2. Journal entry, October 25, 1962.
3. Journal entry, October 1962.

to. "God's callings are God's enabling. Love to Christ is the greatest modifying factor for our bringing men to him."[4] My desire was to bring the word of God to the Chinese people.

> God has given every man an inner witness—the law of God written in the heart to which conscience testifies—and an outer witness—creation. These two combine with the help of the Holy Spirit to give every man enough light so that if he would obey, he would know and walk with God. However, when man rejects and turns his back on this light, he is in darkness. In this state of rejecting the light, he must hear the word of God through which the Holy Spirit will move his heart and show him the way to God through faith in Christ. He must hear the word of God and respond in faith in order to be saved. . . . Thus, it is imperative that we get the gospel to him, which is able to show to him his condition and the way of escape through faith in Christ! "Now faith cometh by hearing, and hearing by the word of God" (Rom 10:17 KJV).[5]

The Lord continued to remind us of his promises, even as he refined our vision for the work to which he called us.

> "*All* power is given unto Me. . . . *Go* ye therefore . . . and, lo, I am with you *alway*" (Matt 28:18–20 KJV).
>
> As the soul is of such tremendous worth, and as there is such an infinite difference between heaven and hell, and whereas the command has been given to go preach in personal word, in life, it behooves us to earnestly and diligently labor to acquire the knowledge of God's word and human nature whereby we can most effectively bring the person or persons to Christ in a born-again relationship. We must give much attention to this skill of leading men to Christ even as we rely on the Holy Spirit continually.
>
> The goal: to build up Spirit-filled, soul-winning, *national leadership*. This I will endeavor to do through Christ.[6]

4. Journal entry, November 1962.
5. Journal entry, January 1963.
6. Journal entry, February, April/May 1963. Emphasis added.

Beside my graduation picture in the ATS 1963 student direc-
tory, I put 2 Tim 1:7 as my favorite Scripture. This verse has a marvelous promise from God which Ruth and I needed as we left for
the mission field that fall: "For God did not give us a spirit of ti-
midity, but a spirit of power, of love and of self-discipline."

After I graduated from ATS,
we began a long road trip pulling
a small U-Haul trailer behind our
car all the way to Seattle, Washington. We served in a church there
that summer, and then spent a few
weeks helping at a beautiful Christian camp just north of Seattle while
we waited for the ship that would
take us to Hong Kong.

The day finally came and we
sailed on a Maersk Line freighter.
It was a month of marvelous pas-
sage—first to Alaska, then to Japan, and finally to Hong Kong.
Ruth was pregnant with our first child, Glenn, so we walked the
deck at various places, the bow being one of our favorite spots. We
ate in the dining hall with the officers of the ship.

> Tomorrow, we arrive at our long-awaited destination—
> Hong Kong. How gracious and faithful is our God! Two
> evenings ago, we saw the most beautiful sunset I have
> ever seen. The afterglow of the setting sun lit up the sky
> and calm sea in dazzling splendor. The water near us was
> purple, farther away toward the sun was radiant silver-
> pink, and the water ahead of the ship was bluish green.
> This was undoubtedly one of the most amazing sights of
> God's handiwork in nature I have ever seen.
>
> This evening God gave another beautiful sight. We
> have been traveling for some time off the coast of China,
> but at a close enough distance, with our fair visibility,
> that some thought they could make out part of the coast,
> but it was exceedingly difficult. However, as the sun set in
> a great perfect disk of red and came down to the horizon,

it illuminated to our vision a point of land that was jutting into the sea from mainland Red China, indicated by the ship captain. The land was in bold outline against the face of the setting sun behind it. Can we not take courage from this object lesson in nature that God has given us? The picture of Red China is uncertain and dim. We wonder what the present and future state of the church of Jesus Christ is there. It is hard to see the outline of what the church has gone through and what it will be in the future. But God bids us take courage. When we view the Chinese church with the eye of faith against the radiant disk of God's power and providence, we know that tomorrow will be a brighter day.

"Upon this rock [Christ Jesus] I will build my church; and the gates of hell shall not prevail against it" (Matt 16:18 KJV).

Another thing Christ showed me today in object lesson. I was admiring the gears on the mechanism at the bow of the boat, which lets the heavy anchors into the sea and draws them up again. Here were different gears, some large, some small; one was vertical, others horizontal; one was huge, but the one that intermeshed and drove it was quite small in comparison. If one of these gears did not work, it could easily make the whole mechanism out of order. Each gear had to do its own work well in order for the job to be done. Each gear was tremendously important and yet depended on the others. Is not this a picture of the church? The job to be done is the building of the kingdom—men and women coming to know Christ as Savior and Lord. We all have an important place to fill in this work, whether it seems big or small. The important thing is that we do our work with a whole heart, efficiently, and this can be done by fully committing oneself to and relying upon the Holy Spirit.

How good is God! How thrilling to be soon in his place of service in Hong Kong. There is no greater experience than to follow Christ and be in his service, wherever He leads us. Our trust is in him.[7]

7. Journal entry, September 1963.

When we finally arrived in Hong Kong in early October, we were warmly welcomed by the colleagues in our mission and local people in our churches and schools. In December 1963, we sent our first prayer letter from Hong Kong to supporters in the United States.

> Dear friends,
>
> Christmas time again—our hearts rejoice with you in this blessed season of the year. We now are on the continent on which the Christ Child was born, yet so few know this message of Bethlehem. How glad we are that we can celebrate this Christmas with our Chinese brethren and proclaim the glad tidings of great joy that unto us has been born a Savior who is Christ the Lord.
>
> We had a very pleasant voyage arriving in Hong Kong on October 1, the day before our language program began. Suitable apartments are very difficult to find here, yet in answer to your prayers [our fellow missionary] found the perfect place for us to live. It is on the ninth floor of a recently constructed apartment house, with elevators . . . on the Kowloon side of Hong Kong in the very hub of activity. We have two large rooftop spaces and are but a few minutes' walk from the meat, vegetable, and fruit shops as well as all other shopping conveniences. From the north side of our apartment can be seen the mountains of the New Territories rising above the city while beyond these lies Communist China. From the south side we view the beautiful harbor of Hong Kong framed against the shoreline of Hong Kong Island. Here by day we see a constant stream of activity, fishing junks, tugboats, barges, sampans, ferries, ocean liners, freighters, and naval vessels all intermingling together as they busily come or go or lay at anchor. Behind this scene of bustling activity stand tall, graceful buildings, yet standing out in sharp contrast to them are thousands of squatter huts clinging to the side of the mountain. One is always aware that this is a city with a vast influx of humanity. When we come from the matchbox-size living quarters of the refugees to our comfortable apartment we wonder why we should have so much and they so little.

The water situation is threatening to become worse. We are on a four-hours-every-four-days schedule and although we don't find it too difficult because of adequate storage space, the Chinese do. In many areas they must line up for hours waiting for the water to come on and then take home only as much as they can carry. The government is aware of the situation and is seeking to do what can be done to relieve it. We were interested to learn the other day that the flagship of the United States Seventh Fleet, which is in port this week, is giving ten thousand gallons of water a day to Hong Kong through its distilling equipment. Freighters which dock in the harbor give their excess fresh water to the cause also.

In walking through the very crowded streets of Hong Kong and looking into the faces of the people we have come to serve, we have felt at such a loss because we cannot communicate with them the message we have come to tell. Our time, therefore, is now taken up in learning the difficult, seven-toned language of Cantonese. Pray for us as we continue studying day after day.

We are anxiously awaiting the arrival of the littlest Winslow. Ruth has kept in good health, remained active, and Harry, too, has stood up well under the strain of expectant fatherhood. The great event is to take place the first week of December in a newly constructed Hong Kong Baptist Hospital by the dedicated missionary, Dr. Rankin. The feeling in the air is one of great expectancy—has not this also been planned and ordained of the Lord?

The past few weeks have been wonderful even though ones of adjustment for us. Christ's promise to be with us has proven itself time and time again. We want to thank you for your sustaining prayers for often in times of testing we have felt that someone at home was lifting us heavenward.[8]

Our first son, Glenn, was chomping to get into the world early. He came on November 26, 1963, and was the first foreign

8. Letter from Harry and Ruth Winslow to friends, December 1963.

baby to be born in the Kowloon Baptist Hospital. What a blessing to have this beautiful baby boy in our family!

Our apartment building sat very near the harbor on the Kowloon side. We could see ocean ships going slowly both ways in the harbor from one of the windows in our tenth-floor apartment. These included the magnificent Queen Elizabeth ship and navy vessels from different countries. Since our apartment was on the top floor, we had the key to the flat rooftop area. It was the perfect place to dry clothes and give baby Glenn some sunshine without having to go to the park.

I first studied the difficult Cantonese language at a language school, then later with a tutor at home. Ruth also studied with a tutor at home. Cantonese normally has six tones, so you must be very careful not only to give the correct sound to a word, but also the correct tone. The same sound with a different tone can mean something entirely different. That can get you into real trouble very quickly! The Cantonese people grow up speaking it so the tones come automatically for them, but not so for foreigners. I finally got to the point where I could preach very elementary sermons in Cantonese.

In the 1950–60s, a large influx of refugees came over the border from Mainland China into Hong Kong. The city did not have enough low-cost housing for these poor immigrants, so many of them lived in densely crowded squatter huts. These were unhygienic and could easily catch on fire, which too often proved deadly for the occupants. To help remedy this, the Hong Kong government built H-block buildings, named for their shape when viewed from above. Built several stories high, many tiny apartments lined the two sides of the H and community bathrooms were located in the middle crossbar. On the flat roof of H-block buildings, school rooms were provided so the children living there could go to school. The government allowed different organizations, including churches, to run the schools. In this way, our Free Methodist church was able to establish two rooftop schools and use the same spaces for Sunday meetings, helping to meet the needs of the people.

Soon another blessing came. Our second son, Mark, was born on October 11, 1965. Our family was growing fast with all the joys that brought. We were delighted that Glenn had a baby brother to play with.

Conference ended yesterday afternoon. . . . Previous few weeks have been hectic. God has stood by. Now is our time to trust and pray as never before. This must be the focus point of our ministry. Here is God's promise: "Behold, God is my salvation; I will trust, and not be afraid: for the LORD JEHOVAH is my strength and my song; he also is become my salvation. Therefore with joy shall ye draw water out of the wells of salvation" (Isa 12:2–3 KJV).

Oh, Lord, grant that this living water may be shared with many others this year as Rebecca gave to Abraham's servant. We thank thee this morning for thy matchless grace. We trust in thee, so guide and direct us that we may be right in the place of service, that kind of service, where you can use us best in spreading the living healing water of thy salvation to the thirsty. Amen.[9]

We had been in Hong Kong about two years when we received a shocking letter from our mission board directing us to move from Hong Kong to Taiwan. They wanted me to teach at the Holy Light Theological College in Taiwan. Cantonese is not spoken in Taiwan, so this would mean we would have to learn another language—the Mandarin that was used in Taiwan. We were not at all eager to do this, having put so much effort into learning Cantonese. I prepared to write a strong letter back to the mission board telling them we should not go.

Right around that time, I was in the shopping section of Hong Kong with a friend. He suggested we get an immunization shot like other people were doing at a place on the street. People were lined up so we stood in line and finally got the inoculation.

Not long after, I noticed strange things happening to me. My eyes became yellow and my urine changed to very dark yellow. I went to see the doctor and found out I had hepatitis B. I had contracted it from that shot on the street. They had not cleaned the needle well enough between patients.

The doctor told me that I could not now work. I had to stay in bed and I could not even read a book. He impressed upon me the seriousness of my situation. He told me about a football player who had contracted hepatitis, didn't listen to his instructions, went out to play football, and dropped dead on the field. I paid close attention to what he said, went straight home to bed, and stayed there. Ruth had to pick up most of the work that I had been doing.

One day, she was climbing the seven stories up to the roof of an H-block building to give the money for teachers' salaries. As usual, the sky was dark with pollution from the city. The Lord

9. Journal entry, May 1965.

49

spoke to her and said, "If you go to Taiwan, you will see clear, blue skies and green mountains." She felt in that moment better about going.

Lying in bed, I had a lot of time to think. I began to feel that I should not write that letter to the mission board. Maybe we actually *should* go to Taiwan. After Ruth came home from the H-block, she shared her thoughts. God had spoken to both of us.

The next time I saw the doctor, about six weeks after my diagnosis, he was amazed that I had almost fully recovered. He said he had never seen such a fast recovery.

Jesus is my Wonderful Counselor. He knew how to stop me, turn Ruth and me around, and set our faces in the direction he wanted us to go. It was like a woven carpet: we only saw the underside of tangled threads, but he could see the beautiful picture unfolding on the other side.

7

God's Hand of Blessing

IF YOU HAVE CLEAR assurance of where God's hand is pointing, then follow through, you will certainly receive his blessing. Rather than going on furlough to the United States after three years in Hong Kong, we decided to go directly to Taiwan. This involved a lot of packing, but we did it, and arrived safely in Taiwan in 1966. My assignment was to teach at Holy Light Theological College, but first I needed to learn Mandarin.

We moved into a house that had been rented for us in Taipei, the capital city, and I began studying Mandarin at the Taipei Language Institute (TLI). Ruth had a tutor who came to our house to teach her. I went by bicycle to and from TLI and little Glenn rode in a small metal seat behind me. I dropped him off at a Chinese preschool on the way and picked him up on my way home. I had very good teachers and made rapid progress in the language. It was our second Chinese language to learn on our first term abroad, but it was somewhat easier than Cantonese since it only had four tones instead of six. I still had to be very careful to get the tones right or I could get in big trouble.

I heard a story about a foreigner who was studying Mandarin in Taiwan and went to visit the mainland. He needed to find out how to get to the train station. He asked a girl on the street for directions. Without saying a word, she slapped him right across the face! "Wow, these people are really fierce," he thought. The problem, however, was his. Two different characters *sound* exactly the same, but they are pronounced with *different* tones. *Wen* 问 fourth tone means "to ask," but *wen* 吻 third tone means "to kiss." He had used the third tone with the polite word *qing* 请 in front of it intending to say, "Please, may I ask a question?" but instead he said, "Please kiss me"!

While we were studying Mandarin, our church leaders in Southern Taiwan decided to send a pastor to start a church in Taipei in the north so that university students from our churches in the south would have a place to worship together. They picked our house as the place to start it. Each week we set up folding chairs in our living room for the worship services.

This period was a difficult time for Ruth and me. We were still in language study and quite busy managing our growing family. Our third blessing, Keith, was born during our first winter there on January 29, 1967. He was an absolute delight, and Glenn and Mark had a little brother to play with. We had a washing machine but no dryer, so diapers and clothes took a long time to dry in our house with the damp, chilly weather outside. It did not help that there was an open water canal just a stone's throw from our house. We had to be vigilant to make sure Glenn, the inquisitive boy that he was, did not go in that direction. Through all the hubbub of life with young children, we continued to study and host the church in our home. I noted in my journal: "Today I preached my first sermon in Mandarin. God was faithful. Praise his name. . . . In the Taipei church on the front of the pulpit is the cross. My prayer when preaching must be, '*Help me, Lord, to hide behind the cross.*'"[1]

I finished my study at TLI in a year and a half rather than the normal two years since I already knew characters from my Cantonese studies. I had a problem though because sometimes I did not know if a spoken word was Cantonese or Mandarin. I finally decided to let my Cantonese go. I certainly did not need it in Taiwan.

1. Journal entry, December 1967

After finishing language school, we moved to Pingtung in the south. We found a good house with a fenced yard which was much safer than the setting in Taipei. Our three sons could now run around freely inside and outside the house.

Our assignment for the next year and a half was to help tribal churches in two annual conferences of our denomination. Over the centuries, the indigenous tribes, the original inhabitants of Taiwan, had been pushed by the Dutch, Chinese and Japanese up into the high mountains. Our church was working with the two tribes located in the south, the Rukai and Paiwan tribes. The Rukai lived in the high mountains while the Paiwan had settled in the lower mountains. The tribal people had been fierce headhunters who would ambush and kill members of the opposite tribe, then take their heads and put them in small cubicles in the stone trophy fence built at the center of their village. Now many members of these two mountain tribes had become Christians. The woman pictured here with Ruth was the mother of two of our Rukai pastors.

Ruth worked in community health, diligently teaching the Rukai mothers how to better care for their children. She also spearheaded development projects including a large, strong swinging bridge.

You can learn more about the work Ruth and I did among these precious mountain tribes in her two books, *The Mountains Sing* and *Love Found a Way*. Suffice it to say

that the mountains where they lived and the people themselves were a delight to work with. Sometimes when I was walking along a mountain trail with an elderly Christian tribesman, I wondered if he had taken heads in his earlier life, but I did not dare to ask.

Our church leaders were wise to send us to the tribal churches in those early days because the tribal people's Mandarin was not as good as the polished Mandarin spoken by the Chinese on the plains. We could practice our Mandarin among them without embarrassment. They had their own tribal languages, so Mandarin was a second language for them as much as it was for us.

One day, Glenn was brought home midday by a teacher from his Chinese preschool. We learned he had been walking on top of the school compound wall during recess, slipped, and fell into the *benjo*, the waste water trough that ran beside the road. His left leg had quite an abrasion. He was crying and crying and wouldn't stop. He was taken to his bed but he kept crying there, too. With all this crying, Ruth decided to look at the abrasion more carefully. As she did so, a bone poked out! It was a compound fracture. Glenn needed a serious operation right away. The Lord then gave us the following three different miracles during this experience.

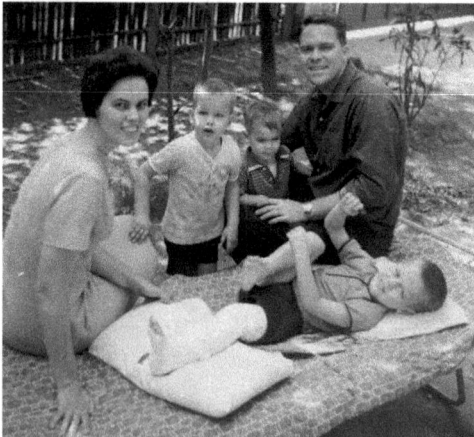

Ruth had been helping an orthopedic doctor from Taipei, Dr. Shen, as he performed surgery on children with scoliosis at the Pingtung Christian Hospital. He had been scheduled to fly back to Taipei that same afternoon, but his plane had been delayed. When he heard about Glenn's injury, he agreed to do the surgery immediately. We had a top-rated surgeon to operate on Glenn's leg.

Since it was a dirty *benjo* wound, Dr. Shen expected it to become infected. That night Ruth went to Glenn's room, laid her hands on the cast, and prayed in the name of Jesus with authority that there be no infection. We learned several days later, when the window on the cast was created, that there was no infection. It was a clean wound.

Dr. Shen had to remove part of the bone during the operation. He explained that Glenn's left leg would be shorter, but when he was older a wedge could be inserted to adjust the length.

When we lived in Hong Kong, Ruth had made friends with an older British lady who walked her dogs in the park where the boys played. When she heard about Glenn's accident, she sent us $500. At first, we thought we might use it to buy a piano, but she insisted we use it to buy toys for the boys. We went to the biggest department store in Kaohsiung and found play metal cars about three feet long. A child could sit in it, push pedals to make it go, and turn a small steering wheel to make it turn. We bought two. Glenn and Mark had great fun for many days, pumping hard with their legs, racing around inside and outside our fence. After a few months, Glenn had an X-ray taken of his leg. His left leg was the same length as his right one because of all the exercise he had gotten pedaling the play car. Praise God!

This picture is not the play car! Mark was on a friend's motorcycle.
Keith was in the back, wishing he could get on too.

Ahh, this is more like it—better together! But who is going to drive?
L–R: Keith, Mark, Glenn.

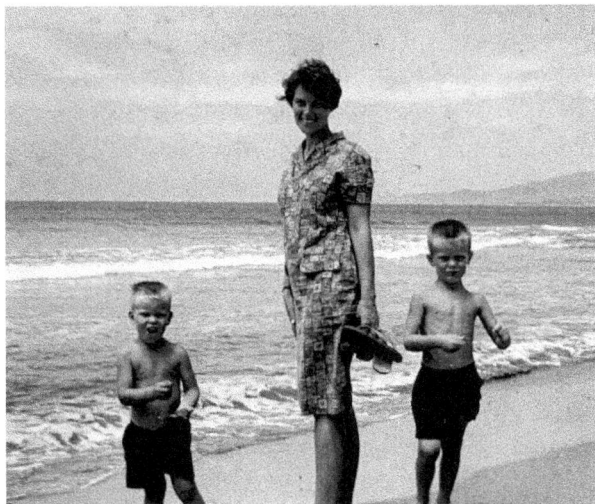

**Our very energetic older two sons, Glenn and Mark, with
Ruth at our favorite beach in Southern Taiwan.**

Yesterday coming back from our trip to Tsau Pu we
stopped on the "Pacific Cliff" overlooking the ocean near
Fang Lyau to eat our picnic supper. The sea was beautiful
in the night and the tide was in. Six-year-old Glenn had
seen it before in daylight, but evidently not at high tide.
He remarked, "It looks like someone put more water in
there!" How great is God! And how small is our compre-
hension of him.[2]

By 1969, it was time to go on furlough. We had been on the
field for six years, three in Hong Kong and three in Taiwan. We
decided to make Greenville, Illinois, our home during furloughs
since we had wonderful friends there from our college days.
Greenville College even had a furnished home for us to rent.

During that year, the mission board sent me to speak in
churches around the United States, sometimes traveling alone for
two or more weeks at a time. Being away from home was not much

2. Journal entry, March 1969.

fun, but sometimes the family came with me. The kids enjoyed the summer camps where Ruth and I spoke.

While we were on furlough, James Hudson Taylor III, the president of Holy Light Theological College (HLTC), contacted me. He invited me to serve as acting president of HLTC because he was moving to Taipei to start a new school, China Evangelical Seminary. I accepted his proposal.

When we returned to Taiwan in 1970, our family moved into the house designated for the president of HLTC in Kaohsiung. This house had been built during the fifty-year span when Japan ruled Taiwan before the end of WWII. We had to get used to the sliding room partitions made from paper attached to wooden frames. If you weren't careful, you could put your finger right through the paper! We came to appreciate it and realized the Japanese design was cooler than most local houses. Right behind our house was a big cement court where the children could play to their hearts' content.

I was acting president at HLTC for one year and then president for four more years until Rev. John Tien, 田養吾牧師 completed his theological studies in the United States and came back to be our first Chinese president.

I am at my desk at the president's office of HLTC where I spent many hours in administrative work and communication with faculty, staff, students, and visitors.

Our forth bundle of joy, Rodney, was born on December 9, 1973 and our family was complete.

Full family picture. L–R: Mark, Harry, Glenn, Rodney, Ruth, Keith.
An earlier May 1970 journal entry: *"Use our family, my precious family you have given me, in your kingdom service; my boys, if it be thy will, for China. Thank you, dear Jesus, for thy love. Amen."*

As United States citizens, Glenn, Mark, and Keith were able to attend the United States Department of Defense elementary school in Tsoying, a town very close to Kaohsiung. This school was constructed for the children of United States Navy personnel who were stationed there. It was a small school, and Glenn's teacher, an elderly lady, was very strict. Glenn was probably a little afraid of her, but it helped him to pay attention better. Glenn and Mark were old enough to play on the school baseball team and had lots of fun. Later, Morrison Academy opened a campus in Kaohsiung, and all of our boys including Rodney attended there.

Eventually, our mission built a house for our family to live close to Kaohsiung. It was two-story, built with reinforced cement, and had a flat roof. This was a great way to build a house there as the cement factory was close, and reinforcement rods were made from old ships being scrapped in the harbor. We installed a large stainless-steel double sink purchased from the resale shop selling items from the ships. Our flat roof had a short wall on four sides and we had it reinforced with a wire fence on top so our kids could play safely there. Ruth and I also enjoyed sitting up there to read, pray, and relax.

Something very unusual happened one day when I was on the roof. I was alone with no one else there and looked up to one side. Suddenly, I saw an object coming horizontally to me with tremendous speed, then it stopped dead in midair not far from me, like it was looking at me. It looked metallic and was about two feet high and five feet long. It did not have wings or any exhaust. After a few moments, it continued its horizontal flight with mind-boggling speed and was out of sight. To this day I do not know what it was, but I'm quite sure it was not an electrical flash from earth or sky, a drone, or a falling star, nor was it a dream or hallucination. I was awake and saw it clearly. One thing is certain—God knows what it was. Maybe later he will let me know.

Ruth and I appreciated being close enough to attend special occasions at my alma mater, Morrison Academy's Taichung campus. In this picture, we are standing on a bamboo walkway made for an event there.

One day Glenn invited Jamie Taylor[3] to come over to our house and showed him a light bulb with a papier-mâché covering he had made in school. Glenn screwed the bulb into a lamp and turned it on for them to see the beautiful sight. They forgot to turn the lamp off, though, when they left the room and the house. The papier-mâché caught fire from the heated bulb, and the fire spread from the lamp to the curtains to the window frame to a wooden cupboard. Only our Amah was home at the time, taking care of little Rodney, who was sleeping upstairs in another bedroom. She smelled smoke, raced upstairs, grabbed Rodney, and fled out to the street. Fire engines came and put out the flames. It had not spread to any other rooms since the door to that one room had been shut.

Where was the rest of the family during this crisis? HLTC commencement was in full swing that day. We had invited a very distinguished speaker, the elderly founder of the school, James Hudson Taylor II, who had flown over from the United States to give the commencement address. He also happened to be Jamie's grandfather! As president, I was sitting on the platform when my assistant came over and handed me a note saying my house was on fire. Not knowing any details, I did not think it required me leaving that august meeting. I indicated that our mission caretaker could handle the situation.

After the meeting concluded, I finally got home and found the window frames in a heap out on the street, partially burned and all wet. Later, I had them scraped, painted, and reinstalled. I was surprised to learn how the fire got started, and so thankful Rodney was safe and that the fire had not spread to the rest of the house. That day we were especially grateful that our house had been built of reinforced concrete instead of wood or else the story might have had a more tragic ending.

Considering the many miles Ruth hiked to serve in the mountains during the years I was at HLTC, sometimes with me

---

3. Jamie was James Hudson Taylor IV, the great-great-grandson of James Hudson Taylor who founded the China Inland Mission. He grew up in Taiwan at the same time as our children.

and some of our boys, it is no wonder that our sons love hiking. There is a small lake set in a deep forest of the high mountains in Taiwan. Few people had visited this remote place, which lent an air of mystery and adventure to it that made our older boys clamor to go. We finally decided to go and gathered a group for a backpacking trip: myself, Ruth, Glenn, Mark, Keith, an American lady, and a Rukai pastor and his friend to guide us. It was a multiday hike, beautiful in many places and gnarly in others where we had to step very carefully and trust God to keep us safe. The picture of me on the next page reveals some of the challenges we faced.

On the way, we pitched our tents by a fork in a stream to get some rest before going on the next morning. It rained that night, and the next morning we learned the Rukai pastor had spent a restless night watching that the water did not rise too high and sweep us away.

We found a small deer caught in a trap set by hunters from another tribe. The tribal people's custom allowed people so far inside the forest to eat animals they found in traps, but they had to carry the head back to the tribe that set the trap. Our mountain guides knew which tribe it was by the design of the trap, so they cut the head off and we had tasty venison to eat to strengthen us. We had a safe trip all the way in and all the way back.

I had to trust God and walk very carefully step by step.

Through the years, we continued to see God's provision for our needs, and appreciated those who prayed for us and supported us in many ways. "Received a Christmas card from the States today which said, 'May God richly continue to bless you each one as you sacrifice for him.' It is not a sacrifice; it is a *privilege*."[4]

> Wonderful promise in my mother's letter which came this morning. Had just been talking with some people regarding problems at HLTC. "When thou goest, thy steps shall not be straitened; and when thou runnest, thou shalt not stumble" (Prov 4:12 KJV). According to

4. Journal entry, November 1974.

Webster, "straiten" means: "to restrict; to hamper, distress or embarrass in means or in condition of life."[5]

An early annual conference of our church in Taiwan had delegates
from three districts. My mother is third from left in the second
row. Geneva Sayre (mentioned in chap. 17) is right beside her. I
am fourth from left in the third row. Mountain tribal delegates
are in the first row. The HLTC building is behind us.

5. Journal entry, July 1975.

8

A New Vision

WHEN WE CAME BACK to the United States in 1976 for our second furlough, we had again been on the field for a six-year term. We rented a spacious, furnished house in Greenville, Illinois, and our four boys all enrolled in school there while I visited churches on weekends. This time, our mission allowed us to stay for two years so I could earn a master's degree in Chinese and Japanese studies at Washington University in St. Louis. I was very interested in finding out what had taken place in China during the terrible unrest that had been going on for nearly a decade. It became known as the Cultural Revolution, which lasted from 1966 to 1976.

During this Revolution, Mao purposely used youth who had been in school to overthrow the educated and landlord classes. Known as Red Guards, they organized into different groups and caused great disturbance and bloodshed across all of China. After this the Red Guard groups began fighting between themselves. To stop it, Mao sent them from the cities and towns to the countryside to toil in the fields. They were not allowed to come back to their schools. They were being rejected by the country's leaders. Most became heartbroken over their plight.

I wanted to write about this lost generation for my master's thesis, but I hadn't been able to find enough material to write about this phenomenon. One of my professors at Washington University had been born and raised in China. He was quite aware of what had happened. Some of the disillusioned youth had begun to write poems and stories in Chinese which became known as "scar literature." He encouraged me to translate several of these stories as my master's thesis. This helped me gain a greater understanding of this formative part of modern Chinese history.

When we went back to Taiwan in 1978, I began teaching again at HLTC. After President Nixon's historic visit to China in 1972, it had become possible for foreigners to visit a few open cities in China. It was like a beautiful spring day after a long, harsh winter.

Even with the new openness, tourism was highly regulated. Guests were required to join a tour and fly from city to city. When they were in a city, they were bussed from site to site and always accompanied by a guide who only took them to carefully selected places. Tourists could exchange United States dollars for Chinese money at their hotel, but it was not the normal currency the Chinese people used. This "funny money" could only be used in hotels or at certain highly regulated shops designated for foreigners.

During this time, I was asked to serve as the interpreter for a tour to Mainland China sponsored by our denomination. We all thoroughly enjoyed the tour. I remember the airline pilot banking the plane to land much more tightly than a normal commercial pilot would have done. I guessed he must have come out of the Chinese Air Force.

All this, fortunately, has now changed. The funny money is long gone. Foreign tourists use standard yuan right along with the Chinese people and pay the same prices. Now many different airline companies fly around China with very good planes and pilots.

With the Lord as your guide, many times you will not know what golden opportunity is right around the corner. Such was the case on this first trip to Mainland China. During the tour, I got acquainted with a gentleman from Kansas who was a wheat farmer. Ervin Brown described his farm operation to me, explaining how he hired extra help during wheat harvest to drive trucks carrying the wheat to the proper destination.

Only God knew at that moment how important this conversation would be. I told Ervin I had four sons, indicating when they were in college maybe they could help him during wheat harvest.

Later this came to pass, and what a great blessing it was—a Christian home to stay in where they were cared for like family; a solid community church for worship; the opportunity to learn the different skills of life on the farm; and good wages to help with college expenses. Over the years, all four of our sons worked different summers on his wheat farm in Kansas.

One other unexpected bonus was that Glenn met his wife, Polly, there. She grew up on a farm near the Browns. Glenn and Polly got married in that little community church, and it all came about because I followed God's direction to have a conversation with a farmer from Kansas on a plane in China.

The Lord began to speak to me during our third term in Taiwan about the need for Christian literature in Mainland China. Besides teaching, I was now the director of a new department at HLTS named Light and Life Communications. Our primary objective was to prepare Christian radio programs for broadcasting into China. As China had begun to open up, we also saw a great need for Christian literature to help the believers in the fast-growing house churches. The Chinese church grew from one million Christians in 1949 to around 100 million Christians in 2025.

With this exponential growth, church leaders desperately needed training and discipleship tools for false doctrines, and cults were sweeping widespread in the country. Besides Christian radio the right kind of Christian literature could be greatly used by God to help meet this pressing need. Books and booklets could be passed from one person to the next and used for years. I needed to move back to Hong Kong.

> Coming home from a meeting, I saw something I had never seen before—a boy was crawling across a very busy street with buses and cars—heavy traffic. He was on hands and knees because of a deformity, about fifteen years old, with a whistle (like a referee's) in his mouth. He was blowing it as he crawled along, hoping the impatient bus/car drivers would notice him and not crush him. China—the church underground, the many who have not heard—need prayer desperately like that crippled boy in such danger needing desperately to be seen. Lord, help me, step-by-step, to be faithful to your vision with understanding, proper balance, and a grasp of the essentials. Amen.[1]

A bishop of our church visited our home in Taiwan around this time. I will never forget his consideration of me. The two of us were sitting together in a room and I was pouring out my heart, telling him about this concern that was so very important to me—I wanted to be reappointed to Hong Kong so I could do literature ministry for Christians in China because of the great need there. After a while it suddenly dawned on me that I was doing all the talking and I apologized to him. He said, "If I had wanted you to stop, I would have told you." What a beautiful example of kindness, listening instead of talking, then giving me such a gracious response.

Praise be to the Lord, after consultations with our mission board in the United States, they agreed that we could move to Hong Kong after finishing the fourth year of our term in Taiwan and then one furlough period.

---

1. Journal entry, December 1978.

PART FOUR

1983–2025

"And he will be called . . . Mighty God."

(ISA 9:6B)

THIS NAME FOR JESUS, Mighty God, resonates over and over in this fourth period of my journey. He is my Mighty God. I can trust him in times of trouble.

9

Back to Hong Kong

IN DECEMBER 1983, IN these excerpts from a letter to our supporters, we reflected on twenty years of ministry, and where we now lived in Hong Kong:

> Twenty years ago, in 1963, we arrived in Hong Kong as young new missionaries. Three years later, according to God's plan, we moved to Taiwan. During three terms of service, we have much to thank God for:
>
> - Studying two Chinese languages, Cantonese in Hong Kong and Mandarin, the national language of China, in Taiwan.
> - Giving Harry a ministry of teaching and administration at Holy Light Theological College in Taiwan.
> - Giving Ruth the privilege of a medical ministry of healing to tribal people in the mountains of Southern Taiwan, and on the plains among those who hurt with leprosy and scoliosis.
> - The opportunity of assisting our Chinese church, both in Hong Kong and Taiwan.
> - Having the joy of four sons coming into our family, Glenn and Mark born in Hong Kong and Keith and Rodney born in Taiwan.
> - Giving Harry a ministry of [preparing] Christian doctrine and Bible studies for new Christians in

China to nurture and strengthen their biblical faith. It is because of this priority ministry that God has now brought us back to Hong Kong after seventeen years away.

We arrived in August and first lived in a leave apartment in Kowloon. The Lord led us to an excellent apartment in Taikoo Shing, on the east side of Hong Kong Island, where we moved in November. Taikoo Village is a city within a city, where 80,000 people will be able to live in a six-block-long by three-block-wide area! Over fifty tower buildings, each twenty-eight to thirty stories high, will rise into the sky when fully completed. We live on the seventh floor of our building. From our windows we can see and hear a panorama of sights and sounds: oceangoing vessels mingle with barges, tugboats, Chinese junks, yachts, and graceful ferries on the undulating water of the harbor; huge jets, almost at our eye level, as they approach the airport runway; down below us on the street the throb of humanity—double-decker buses, taxis, cars, people walking.[1]

The following spring, in April 1984, we described a difference in seasons in another prayer letter:

Where we live in Hong Kong, spring is depicted not by the robin, but by billowing, white fog rolling in from the ocean down the harbor channel. You see it from our apartment as it slowly comes, changing the busy waterway into a fairy wonderland. Here the masts of one or two ships, there the forms of others as they glide by, an ever-changing, beautiful sight. They seem to play hide-and-seek with the fog. The sound of foghorns, of different pitch and tone, answer each other through the mist. Very recently, one freighter sank near the approach to the harbor after being rammed by another ship in heavy fog. How important it is to know that we who believe in Christ have the One who created the universe to chart and guide our lives.[2]

1. Letter from Harry and Ruth Winslow to friends, December 1983.
2. Letter from Harry and Ruth Winslow to friends, April 1984.

I began a very rewarding ministry to Christians in China presented in chapters 10 and 11. Ruth began her amazing medical ministry inside China as told in her autobiography. Glenn, Mark, and Keith were now at Morrison Academy Boarding School in Taichung, Taiwan. Rodney commuted from home to the Hong Kong International School. Later in junior high this school became prohibitively expensive so Rodney got special permission to enter Morrison Academy Boarding School at a younger age than others for his older brothers had set a good record there.

Our boys were excellent students and participated in a lot of extracurricular activities including sports, choir, and band. Both Glenn and Mark played at the same time on the varsity basketball team. I remember when Ruth and I were in Taiwan how excited and hyped they were about flying to Hong Kong with the team for a regional basketball tournament!

One event we all enjoyed was the school musical. When we were in Taiwan, Ruth and I would drive up from Kaohsiung to attend these if any of our boys were performing in the play. Our favorite one was *Fiddler on the Roof*. Glenn, Mark, and Keith were all actors in that one. Glenn, as a senior, had the leading role of Tevye, the father. He performed his part very well, and I still remember him singing with great gusto while dancing "If I Were a Rich Man." Ten years later, the school put on the same play and Rodney, a senior by then, played Tevye. Ruth and I flew over from Hong Kong to see his wonderful performance.

Lantau Mountain became one of our favorite vacation spots in Hong Kong. A Christian retreat center had been built on the top of the ridge, and in the hot summer missionary families often went up there to escape the sweltering heat of the city and enjoy the spectacular views.

I had the privilege of giving the baccalaureate message when Glenn graduated from Greenville College and Mark was a junior. The title of my message was "World-Class Christians for World-Class Cities." Here is an excerpt:

I remember our son Mark's reaction when he visited us in Hong Kong. He was a bit uneasy to find so many people were living right above and below us, about seven hundred above and two hundred below. Hong Kong, more than anything else, is people. It is one of the most densely populated areas on earth. It is the people that make the city. A city without people is meaningless! Look down the city sidewalk during business hours and you see an unending sea of people, black heads bobbing. Hong Kong is people! Throngs of people, multitudes of individuals, each one precious in God's sight.[3]

3. Winslow, "World-Class Christians," baccalaureate message, Greenville College, Greenville, Illinois, May 1986.

In 1988, Ruth and I received the Greenville College Parents Award for "the positive, supportive influence of [our] Christian home." L–R: Mark, Rodney, Ruth, Harry, Glenn, and his wife, Polly.

My incredible wife, Ruth, is God's goodness to me. Prettier than the Chinese silk screen. She has strong faith in God which carries her through the tough times.

Since she was trained and certified as a nurse in the United States, she would not be permitted to work in the British medical system of Hong Kong. How would she use her medical skills in our new home there? It didn't take long before she began exploring ways to serve in Mainland China, starting with teaching English to nurses in Guangzhou. You can read about her amazing medical ministry in China in her book *Love Found a Way: The Story of a Nurse in China.*

How do you illustrate love? One way is to use Chinese characters. There are two types: the traditional style which is still used in Taiwan today, and the simplified style which is used in Mainland China and is easier to read and write.

TRADITIONAL CHINESE   SIMPLIFIED CHINESE

These two characters both represent love (*ai*), but there is a striking difference. Right in the middle of the traditional character is the radical 心 (*xin*) meaning "heart." It even looks like a beating heart. In the middle of the simplified character is a flat line 一 with only one bump in it. It looks like the flat line of a monitor when the heart has just died. Both of these characters read "love," but what a difference between the two!

This vivid picture represents Ruth's story. She put the beating heart back into the character for love. "By this all men will know that you are my disciples, if you love one another" (John 13:35).

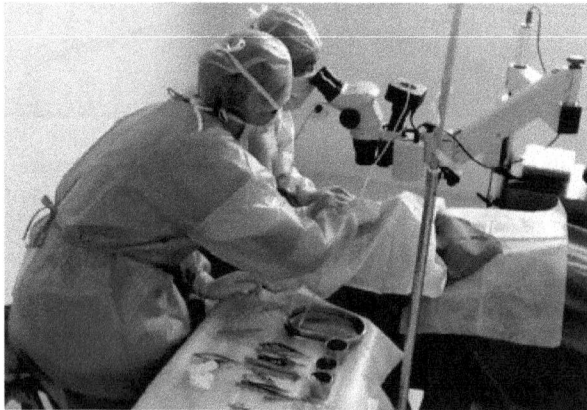

Ruth is in the foreground helping the doctor who is performing eye surgery on a patient suffering from leprosy in Mainland China.

After years of study and writing my dissertation, I received the doctor of missiology degree from Trinity Evangelical Divinity School on June 12, 1993. I had taken courses from Trinity in Taiwan and during two furloughs at their Deerfield, Illinois, campus. The title of my unpublished dissertation was "A People for His Name: A Study of Factors Behind the Rapid Growth of the House Church Movement in China, 1958–1992."

The abstract at the beginning of the major project describes the scope of my paper:

> Much has recently been written on the church in China under Communism. The story of the explosive growth of the house church movement, and the growth, nature, and complexities of the government-sponsored Three-Self Patriotic Movement Church (TSPM), has basically been told. What has not been sufficiently investigated is the question "Why?" Why has this amazing resurrection of the church in China and its rapid growth taken place?
>
> This study endeavors to answer that question. It centers on primary factors behind the rapid growth of the house church movement in China from 1958 through 1992. The term "house church" is used to refer to a local group of Christians who meet regularly, normally in one of the homes of their members. The focus is on the nonregistered house churches, those which have not registered with the TSPM. Thus it does not include a

77

specific study of the TSPM, but the TSPM is mentioned in relation to the house church movement.

Considerable attention is given to the testimony of the New Testament church in the word of God. This testimony is both the antecedent and the best interpreter of much that has happened in the house church in China today.

Sources include interviews with house church leaders inside China; letters from Christian radio follow-up ministries; discussions with Chinese Christians in Hong Kong who came from China; dialogue with people in China ministry; and books, magazine and newspaper articles, and reports giving insight into what God is doing in China today.

The research is organized around six key structural components behind the rapid growth of the house churches in China. These six components are the theological, political, sociological, spiritual, ecclesiastical, and missiological factors which underlay the amazing growth.

Such research is valuable for it can: (1) help us to better understand what God is doing in China today; (2) enable us to pray more intelligently and effectively for the evangelization of China; (3) show us in greater depth what the needs of the house church Christians are and how these needs may be met; (4) provide a model, a case study of church growth factors, which may be analyzed and adapted for greater growth of the church outside China; and (5) encourage and strengthen us in suffering for the name of Christ.

Christians worldwide face mounting persecution as society becomes increasingly secular under the gradual emergence of a one-world economic order. The story of how Christians have become triumphant under persecution in China speaks pointedly and vividly to Christians everywhere who now suffer for the name of Christ, or who will be called upon to suffer in the near future.

So much to praise God for! He is faithful! A marvelous, important truth from God's word today—2 Cor 3:5 ("Not that we are competent in ourselves to claim anything for ourselves, but our competence comes from God.")

The Hallelujah chorus—what a blessing to listen to a tape of the SJ Broadcast (performed in China). This is where it is at! For *that* glorious day we labor! That is our *aim*! Our focus, our reason for life! Hallelujah! Emmanuel![4]

4. Journal entry, March 1996.

10

Many Times Over

AGAIN AND AGAIN, GOD answered prayer when it was most needed. His miracles and wonders happened many times over. When we traveled to many places to teach biblical courses to house church leaders in China many precautions have to be taken. This was because the house churches were not a part of the Communist-government-sponsored churches. If the Police had found us they would have arrested us. I use the language of the people when I teach, which is Mandarin. We do not go to sites we select; we go to sites house church leaders select. If we are coming to a site before evening, we often wear hats so non-Christian people near us cannot clearly see us. We usually arrived after dark so as not to attract attention as foreigners.

I was with an American brother in the far north where we were teaching a good class of students. Suddenly, the two of us were told by the leader to get into a motorized three-wheeler. We hopped in and the driver, who was a believer, immediately took off. He drove to a city some distance away and we rented a place to temporarily stay. Our luggage came to us in another vehicle. What had been the problem? Authorities had come to visit the site where we were teaching. The people in charge of the training had acted quickly.

Another time, I was teaching at a gathering of pastors in the countryside. They had posted a believer down the road from the building who would phone in case of an unexpected visitor. This time I was in my room when suddenly I was told to go from my room to another place in the building. The watchman had called. I quickly went down to the kitchen in the back. I notice a marsh just beyond the kitchen door and wondered if I should run outside into the water and hide behind bushes there. Then a message came that the officials had driven on down the road without stopping. God's grace became very evident in times like that.

One night, I was traveling by taxi with a brother to a meeting place. The taxi driver was not a Christian, so the brother and I were being careful what we said. We continued driving for quite some time into the night. Suddenly, we hit something on the road, swerved to the side, and stopped just before we completely went into a ditch. The car was at a steep angle. I was in the back seat and could not get my door open. There was danger that police might come to check our accident or that gas might be leaking and explode. The driver and the brother up front were able to crawl out a window, but I was too big to do that. Soon other people stopped their cars and came over to see what had happened. They looked in the window at me. I kept my head down and did not say a word. My door was finally yanked open and I was able to crawl out. We had hit cement bricks that were being used to finish the shoulder of the road. They had been left on the road instead of being put to the side. In the dark, our driver had not seen them in time to swerve out of the way. The unexpected had happened, but God was watching over us. We were able to get another taxi and continued on our way.

I was invited to teach at a gathering for house church leaders. I was waiting in the room where luggage bags had been put on a bed. All at once, the leader came in and told me to quickly lie down among the bags. Then he pulled a thick winter blanket completely over me. I did not know what was wrong, but I knew God was with me and I trusted him. After a while, the leader came back. "Can I get up?" I whispered. "No, no," he said and went back out. I stayed under the blanket and continued to trust God. The leader finally came back and said I could get up. He explained that an unbeliever had unexpectedly come to measure the circumference of the building so it could be sold. That was why they wanted me to hide to make sure he didn't accidentally see me.

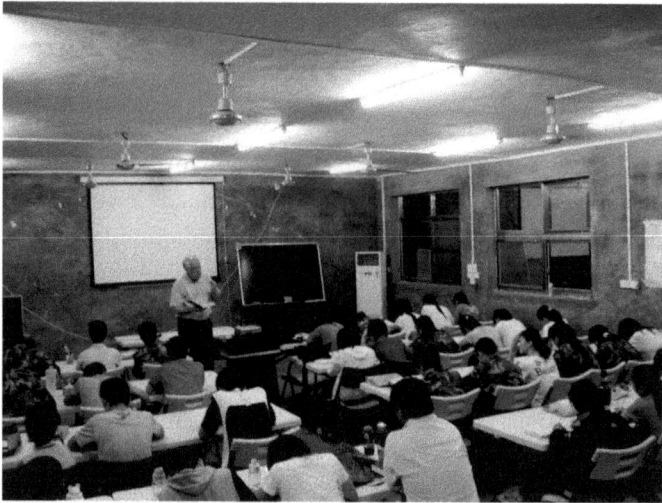

I am teaching a class where many students are house church pastors.

I usually only accepted invitations to teach from people I knew quite well, but one time I was invited by someone I did not know that well. It was actually a case of mistaken identity. I thought he was one of the leaders I knew, but it turned out he was a student who had taken a class from me.

When I arrived, I realized it was a site I had never visited before. Beyond the classroom was an area where believers could come and pray. Some of the people going to pray stopped to see what was going on in the classroom and saw me teaching a class of about thirty people. This should never have happened.

Later, while I was teaching, an alarm went off and everyone immediately rushed for the door, including myself. In the rush, my glasses were smashed against my face, but I got out, quickly made it to my room, and locked the door. Thankfully, my glasses were not broken. I waited and prayed.

Someone came and knocked loudly on my door. I did not know who it was, but I had to open it. Thankfully, it was the leader of the site who told me to leave all my things and come quickly. They would bring my luggage to me later.

I got into a motorized three-wheeler and we took off at a fast pace. We drove for some distance before coming to a believer's house where I ate supper and I stayed for the night. When my luggage was brought to me, I learned that some students had stayed in the classroom to conduct a normal meeting when the authorities came to investigate. The authorities then left, but the believers were afraid they might come back after driving a short distance away. The next day I was able to go on my way without incident. God brought me through this trial, and I was more careful about where I went after that.

Once when I was traveling by myself, I arrived at the site before evening, so I got out of the taxi with my hat on and walked slowly, somewhat hunched over like an old man. When I was teaching inside the building, I stood straight and tall. It was also daylight when the time came for me to leave a few days later. I had to walk a short distance to the taxi waiting for me on the street. I donned my hat again and hunched my shoulders, then walked slowly down the street. A sister who had joined my classes came over to me and said quietly, "*Ni hen ke ai*," which means, "You are very lovable." I just smiled at her and kept walking slowly with my shoulders hunched. I got to the taxi safely!

I was translating for a small group visiting from the United States. We were meeting with a house church evangelist and a few of his coworkers. I asked the evangelist if they had ever experienced miracles. He affirmed, "There are very many. It happens all the time." Then he pointed to a sister and said, "This sister here was run over by a truck, but she got up and was not hurt."

Most of the people in the countryside house churches were poor. They did not have enough money to get good treatment at hospitals. They knew God heard their prayers, so they prayed and God answered with healing many times over. Their simple faith was amazing and inspiring.

Ruth and I occasionally took our boys with us when we went into China to deliver Christian literature. On one occasion, I arranged for a dear brother from Hong Kong who had served God well to go on the first leg of our journey. I did not want the children to know who he was as we traveled on the train and he sat near us. That would be better for security as he was going to help us with book delivery to Christians in the house church.

Our family successfully carried all the books through customs scattered in our luggage. We arrived at our first destination and rented a hotel room for the night. The plan was for our Hong Kong brother to come to our room at a certain time that evening and pick up half the books.

The less expensive hotels in China at that time were modeled after Russian hotels. Each floor consisted of one long hall with rooms on either side, and next to the stairs at the end sat one or two attendants who monitored the traffic up and down the stairs and the hallway. We knew that when our friend came, he would not be carrying anything, but when he left our room, he would have two big sacks of books. That would be dangerous.

We prepared the books for him and waited. He knocked at our door and I welcomed him in. We prayed together for his protection. We knew it could be very difficult for him to get down the stairs without being questioned, but we committed him to our Father's care.

When we opened the door for him to leave, we found the hallway completely changed: a huge amount of steam filled the hall and people were running all about. It was a miracle! During the short time he was with us in our room, the hot water boiler which supplied our whole floor had blown a gasket. It happened at just the right moment! Our friend carried his two big sacks peacefully along the hall and down the stairs without anyone paying him any attention.

Our family continued our journey to deliver the rest of our books to house church Christians in another city. We were in a large train station. Tickets had been bought and we were now sitting in a row of seats like everybody else in a large room. Hundreds of people were waiting for the arrival of the train.

As I examined the tickets more closely, I was unsure whether certain numbers referred to the train car number or our seats inside the train. I saw a train attendant nearby, so I walked over and asked him. I soon found out I should not have done that. Within minutes, a high-ranking official came into the room. He ignored everyone else and walked directly to us. He declared that he had to check our bags for explosives.

We each had our bag on the floor in front of us all along the row. Ruth was at one end and Rodney was at the other, with me beside him. The official began with Ruth, opening and checking each bag along the way. I knew Rodney's bag was the only one with the books. If the official found them, we could be in serious trouble and our visas to come back into the country could be revoked. We silently prayed and leaned heavily upon the Lord.

When he finally came to Rodney's bag, the first thing the official saw was a case of metal Matchbox cars and trucks on the top. He was mesmerized. He kept picking them up and looking at them one by one. He obviously had never seen anything like them before. He never looked any further down in the bag and finally left. God was with us, and I learned a valuable lesson to be more careful to whom I spoke Mandarin!

11

Literature Ministry

SOME OF THE GREAT advantages of books are that they do not need a passport, or visa, or airline ticket to get to the people who need them. They also do not need to spend multiple months learning a very difficult language to be effective. It has been my privilege to help in producing the following Mandarin language Christian literature for use in China. I believe the greatest contribution and legacy I have made to the kingdom of God is the twelve books, one booklet, one graph, and one tract that I detail in this chapter.

TEACHING MANUALS

Church Overview, Part 1 (教会面面观上)

Many Chinese Christians do not understand the identity of the church, resulting in disunity and fractures. Pastors sometimes run the church like an emperor where everyone must listen only to them. Because of this here are two books that give Chinese leaders a comprehensive theology of the church.

Church Overview, Part 1 gives a basic understanding of the first two of five primary relationships of the church—the church and God, and the church and pastors. This clearly portrays who the church belongs to and includes studies on important scriptural terms for the church. It speaks about the spiritual qualifications of the ministry: suffering for Christ, preaching the whole council of God, pastoring the flock, servant leader management, and faithful stewardship. It gives instruction regarding the meeting and ceremony of baptism, the Lord's Supper, Christian weddings, and funerals.

Church Overview, Part 2 (教会面面观下)

Church Overview, Part 2 gives a basic understanding of the last three of five primary relationships of the church—the church and members, the church and the world, and the church and glory. It includes studies on the work of the Holy Spirit, the unity of the body, evangelism, the authority of the believer, recognizing cults, and the church triumphant.

Guard Against and Refute Cults (防备辩驳异端)

With the rapid expansion of the church, many Christians only have a very basic understanding of the gospel. This gives room for false teachers who easily lead naïve believers away from biblical truth. The Eastern Lightning cult even says that Jesus has already returned, but this time he has come as a woman. This manual helps believers discern and refute such false teachings.

Guard Against and Refute Cults builds understanding on how to detect and refute cults. It presents the "plumb line" of biblical truth regarding God, salvation, and the Bible by which all cults can be measured. With biblical teaching and warnings against cults, it also includes practical helps in dealing with any cult and distinguishes between cults, extremism, preferences, and orthodox faith. This book also exposes the major indigenous and imported cults in China at the time of its writing.

Victory Over Spiritual Conflicts (战胜属灵争斗)

This is a very practical, basic course which presents the Christian worldview of Scripture and compares it to the animistic worldview and the Western worldview. It deals with spiritual warfare relationships in the realms of God, angels, and man in the battle for the mind. This course shows how to obtain victory in Christ over demonic activity.

Many of the above manuals were later revised by the training group with whom I worked closely. They became part of the core training materials for house church pastors, leaders, and Bible school students in China.

Enter the 95/25 Big Door (进 95/25 大门)

God has given the Chinese church a vision to share the gospel with Muslims in Central Asia and the Middle East. I explain this powerful vision in chapter 17 when I share the story of Mark Ma. To introduce a new generation of Christian believers to this critical vision, here is the book *Enter the 95/25 Big Door*.

In August 2007, I articulated the significance of this training manual in our prayer letter:

> We praise God that a brand-new cross-cultural mission course in Mandarin has been printed and is being widely taught to pastors and church leaders. This teaching manual's central theme is to help the Chinese church with the vision of sending Chinese missionaries to reach the Muslim world for Christ in what we are calling the Big Door area, which extends from 95 to 25 degrees longitude and 10 to 40 degrees latitude. This is the central part of the 10/40 Window and extends from Western China and Eastern India to Western Turkey and Western Egypt. The Big Door, which includes China and thirty other countries, represents the largest mass of Muslim people groups in the world. A surprising number of these groups have very few or no Christians at all. A great deal of work

has gone into writing and editing this teaching manual. We praise God that it is now being effectively used.

Unlike a window, which is made to look through, a door is made to walk through. We believe the Lord is saying to today's Chinese church: "I know your deeds. See, I have placed before you an open door that no one can shut" (Rev 3:8). God has placed an open door for Chinese missionaries to walk through to take the gospel to the Muslim world. God has uniquely prepared the Chinese church for this task . . . to preach the gospel in Northwest China, then in Central Asia, and then on to the Middle East.

1. Pray that the Holy Spirit will move upon the Chinese church to take up the challenge God gave her more than sixty years ago to take the gospel west to Central Asia and the Middle East.

2. Pray that the Chinese church will effectively reach the many Muslim groups within her own borders, most of whom have very few or no Christians.

3. Pray that the Holy Spirit will show an awakened Chinese church how to partner with Christians who have a Muslim background. These Christians can become effective team members in evangelizing Muslim people groups within the Big Door area. There are a number of Muslim people groups within China who speak the same language and have similar cultures to their own ethnic people groups in countries bordering Western China.

4. Pray that adequate planning and preparation will go into mission training for Chinese missionaries to the Big Door area in order that they will become effective communicators of the gospel.

5. Pray that every copy of the cross-cultural mission manual will be greatly used by God. Not everyone who reads it will study it in class.[1]

1. Letter from Harry and Ruth Winslow to friends, August 2007.

STUDY BIBLE

Useful Study Bible (圣经研用本)

It was my privilege to serve as the general editor of this rich volume. In the production of this study Bible, different groups provided excellent contributions which made it particularly helpful for traveling pastors to carry when they traveled from place to place. It was also very helpful for stationary pastors and Christian leaders to share the truth of the gospel of our Lord Jesus Christ. It includes the complete Union Bible (和合本), which is the preferred Bible of Christians all over China, as well as many helps for studying and sharing. Even with 2,110 pages, it was less than two inches thick because it was printed on very thin paper. It clearly lives up to its literal Chinese title—"the Bible to study and use."

HYMNAL

Everybody Sing (大家歌唱) 大宓(家)歌唱

Based on a handmade hymnal used in China, *Everybody Sing* brought together songs which were especially meaningful to Chinese believers. Nearly two-thirds of the one thousand songs were taken word for word from Scripture or based on Scripture passages; over half of the songs are set to Chinese indigenous tunes which made them easier for Chinese people to learn; and a good number of songs were written by house church Christians, reflecting the "sound of their heart" in their praise to God and trust in him. Printed on thin Bible paper in compact format, the whole hymnal could fit into a shirt pocket. You can read more about how this hymnal developed in chapter 16.

The title of this hymnal was also significant. The first character, 大 (*da*), means "big," and the second character, 家 (*jia*), means "house." When put together, these two characters mean "everybody." House church Christians created a new character for 家 (*jia*) that was used on the cover of this hymnal. They pronounce it the same way, but it is not found in any dictionary, so a non-Christian would not understand its meaning. It is composed of three parts—two Chinese radicals and a character—the 住 top radical 宀 means "roof," the bottom left radical 亻 means "man," and the bottom right character 主 means "Lord." These three parts put together give a much richer meaning than the original character for "house," which is composed of a roof and a pig, a prized possession in ancient China. These house church Christians wanted to emphasize that a house is where people and the Lord live together. What a beautiful way of using this newly created character to express the truth of God's word, "'They will call him Immanuel'—which means 'God with us'" (Matt 1:23b).

SPIRITUAL BOOKS

Grace and Peace (恩平)

A type of catechism with three parts, *Grace and Peace* includes twenty-one important biblical doctrines, 215 questions and answers on truth, and sixty-three pages of songs from *Everybody Sing*.

The Beloved (蒙愛的人)

The title of this book comes from Col 3:12 (KJV) where Christians are described as "beloved"; in the Chinese Bible it is "蒙愛的人." This is a 631-page composite of five books: *Putting Down Roots* (the inner life of the Christian), *Commentary on Ephesians* (the outer life of the Christian), *Commentary on 1, 2, and 3 John* (the fellowship of the Christian), *Commentary on 1 and 2 Peter* (the refinement of the Christian in suffering), and *Night Ends Bright Sky* (the hope of the Christian in Christ's return).

Written in simple Chinese, it can be easily understood by poorly educated farmers or villagers. It was structured to help new believers develop their spiritual life through self-study. There are three book sizes with the same content: regular book size; half book size (that can fit in a shirt pocket); and half book size divided into eighteen booklets (which can individually fit in letter envelopes). There is also a digital download.

Because many copies had been printed with blue covers, the following remarkable correspondence excerpts call it the "little blue book."

Not long ago, a coworker wrote my son: "Hi! I want to introduce a friend to you. . . . She knows who your dad is, and in the past when she and her husband lived and worked in the mainland for a while she often used your dad's little blue book to give to people with whom she shared the gospel. Today she mentioned that it was one of the best discipleship tools she has run across and was wishing she had a copy for herself. . . . Is there a way she can get a copy?" After receiving a copy, the friend wrote me:

> I am very thankful to have received the little blue book—
> 蒙愛的人. I have been thinking about this little blue
> book for twenty years and I received it on my birthday.
> I consider it a very special birthday gift from our Lord.
>
> I had a very special dream. In the dream I asked
> Jesus how much I should contribute towards this little
> blue book reprinting. God gave me this verse instead.
> "When your words came, I ate them; they were my joy
> and my heart's delight, for I bear your name, O Lord
> God Almighty" (Jer 15:16). I woke up and thought that I
> should contribute [around $2,000]. Yet I waited upon the
> Holy Spirit's further confirmation.
>
> The next day, I received in the mail a check . . . which
> was the payment of my speaker fee for a talk in relation
> to Israel. . . . I in fact was not an expert of Israel. . . . I
> prayed to Jesus and said that "Jesus, if you are the Holy
> One of Israel, give me the opportunity to present a talk
> in relation to Israel, *but* it must be a *paid* talk." This was
> such a fearful and joyful experience indeed.
>
> God gave me a very comforting promise (Rom 8:17)
> in relation to this "little blue book ministry" in my daily
> devotion this morning. . . . What a privilege to be joint-
> heirs with Christ to be into [*sic*] this "little blue book

ministry" transforming all suffering into [*sic*] glory! We all *who* get involved are real 蒙愛的人!

In the end, this sister saved around $2,000 she received for her speaking for reprinting the little blue book—蒙愛的人.

The Beloved Handbook (蒙愛的人课程手册)

This book teaches how to develop sermons using *The Beloved* as a basis for twenty-two expository sermons and sixteen topical sermons. It is also an excellent tool for group study of *The Beloved*.

Bible Story Picture Book (圣经故事画册)

Written at a third-grade level with full-page color pictures, this book includes 150 stories that children and adults alike can enjoy.

EVANGELISM MATERIALS

Interesting Bible Stories (趣味圣经故事)

This sixty-five-page story Bible was developed for evangelism. It was written at a sixth- to ninth-grade level, suitable for adults as well as youth. It can also be used by pastors in preaching.

Jesus My Savior (耶稣我救主)

This booklet has many line-art drawings illustrating Scripture passages.

Salvation's Historical Journey Graph (救赎历程简的图解)

This graph has twenty full-color pages of drawings, explanations, and Bible verses giving the historical timeline of salvation from

Genesis to Revelation. The red blood line begins with Adam being driven out of the garden of Eden and goes all the way to the cross. The golden line begins with the resurrection of Christ and goes all the way to the new heaven and the new earth. When folded, it is small enough to fit inside a shirt pocket. When unfolded, it forms a long banner which can be hung on a wall as a visual aid.

Jesus Said (耶稣说)

This small tract has Scripture verses regarding Jesus as the Way, the Truth, and the Life (John 14:6).

12

Family Connections

WHILE WE WERE LIVING in Hong Kong in 1997, my brother, Paul, and his wife, Karen, brought several of their adult children with them to visit China. Ruth, Keith, and I joined them on a journey to revisit our roots. We saw iconic places like the Great Wall in Beijing, but the most memorable part of our trip was traveling to where we had lived as boys in the Henan Province.

Our family had left China in 1941 and returned to the United States to seek medical treatment for my father's severe illness. Only three years old at the time, I have no memories of that place, but my brother was five and did remember China.

We knew the right province—Henan—and the right city— Qixian—but how would we find our boyhood home? Fifty years had passed and we did not know anyone there anymore. Paul remembered that we had lived very close to the church building, so we hired a van with a Chinese driver. I explained what we were looking for and off we went.

The driver took us to a little country church with rough, backless benches. A service was in progress. When the people saw us, they immediately stopped the service and asked us—total strangers—to preach. Paul preached and I interpreted. We realized this was not the church we were looking for, but God had given us an opportunity to minister to these brothers and sisters. At the close of the service, a sister told us she knew the church we were looking for in Qixian. She joined us in the van and led us to the correct place.

This one was a newer, large church which had been constructed on the grounds where the original Free Methodist church had been. We didn't want to interrupt the service in progress there, so Paul and I decided to walk around to see if we could find our old home. We did not find the house, but as we wandered, a group of children and a few adults gathered around us, curious about this strange phenomenon of two, big white men walking down their streets. Then they realized I could speak Mandarin. Suddenly, a man turned to me and motioned toward Paul asking, "*Ta shi bu shi Baoluo?*" (Is he Paul?) I was flabbergasted. How did this man, a complete stranger, know my brother's name was Paul?

We soon learned that he had played with Paul as a young boy. Now some fifty years later, he must have seen in Paul a resemblance to our dad. "Come with me," he urged. "There is someone I want you to meet." Who could it be? We did not have a clue.

As we came back around to the front of the church, an elderly lady with a cart was selling refreshments on the street side. "This lady knew you, Paul," our guide explained. She had been Paul's *amah*, (nanny) who helped take care of him when he was a little boy. She cried when she met Paul. What a marvelous wonder it was to see the little boy she had cared for so long ago! We arrived in the city as strangers, but God arranged in a wonderful way for us to meet long-lost family friends.

13

Retired But Not Out of Service

RUTH AND I RETIRED from career missionary service when I turned seventy in 2008. My coworkers in the Bible teaching ministry in China threw me a retirement party I will never forget.

We were in a large building in Mainland China when the leader of our group came to me and said urgently, "Quick, follow me!" By his tone of voice and manner, it sounded like danger was at hand, so I quickly followed him through the open window he directed me to. "It must be really urgent if we skipped the door!" I thought. We hurried away from the building walking at a fast clip along the forest path, and he kept saying we must go quickly.

Suddenly, I heard a commotion in the bushes. It was my fellow teachers! They were waiting for us to come and give me a surprise party.

They then gave me a great gift for me to take home. It was a very interesting commemorative album of pictures and farewell messages. On the front page they had a very creative picture they had compiled. In the style of a vintage Chinese poster of factory workers they had me standing between three of my fellow coworkers (not shown here). I am posed mid-speech, making a very important point as I hold the Bible in my hand. At the bottom in big red Chinese characters like a slogan it gave the essence of what I was saying: "大学大用神給我们奇妙的圣经," which means "Study a Lot, Use a Lot, the Marvelous Bible God Has Given Us."

Inside the album were words of blessing and gratitude from my coworkers.

Here are two of the messages:

> Congratulations on reaching this significant milestone in your service to our Lord. Your life has been a model of dedication, tenacity, godly integrity, humility, and joyful service to others. Thank you for the resolve to live a life of faithfulness, so far! And, by the look of things, we are not expecting you to live any differently. ☺ Keep it up and keep on.
>
> You have played a significant role in the life of the . . . team even prior to its inception. You were part of the original board of directors when we incorporated in July 1996 and served as our chairman of the board until . . . December 2007. Prior to the start . . . you were instrumental in turning our attention from an urban work, using translated materials from the North American church, to focus on the explosive and dynamic rural church, using newly created materials made with China's rural church in mind.
>
> This seemed like an overwhelming challenge at first, but you threw in your lot with us and have helped contribute to that very curriculum you dreamed would one day come into being. You have been with us, marching in lockstep all the way. Thanks to you, our team has

been able to offer the church in China your five books: *Church Dynamics, Parts 1 & 2*; *Guard Against and Refute Heresy*; *Resolving Spiritual Conflicts*; and *Entering the 95/25 Window* (Big Door).

It has been a precious honor serving our Lord together with you. You have taught me much and encouraged me often. You have always been gracious and kind in your counsel and advice. I am deeply indebted to you.

I must also place in this record how God used Ruth to dramatically influence and alter my life. . . . Thank you, Ruth, for listening to God, and for drawing me back in to China.

You have both used your lives in loving service to leave a lasting legacy for the kingdom of God. Thank you for living your lives well. May God continue to open doors of service for you, to His glory and honor.

On another page was an acrostic with my last name, printed over my face in the background.

What a treasure to have this album with kind words and pictures to take home as a reminder of the many years we had

Wilful obedience to the Lord

Intelligent and insightful

Noble man of integrity and worth

Spry – dancing on the mountains with the help of hornets

Loves God, his family and the Chinese church

Oak of righteousness (Is 61:3)

Walks with God

served the Lord together. I owe any success to God's grace and my dependence upon him.

After forty-five years of full-time missionary service, Ruth and I retired to our home in Greenville, Illinois.

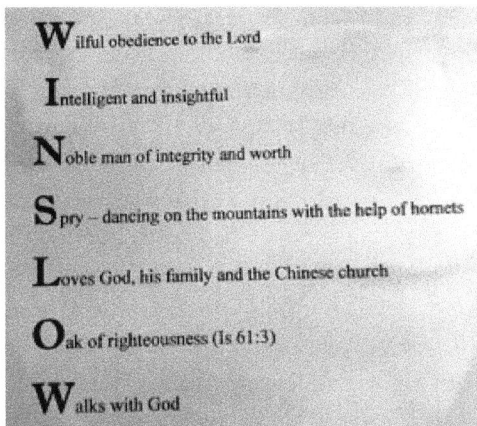

NOT OUT OF SERVICE

For the first few years following official retirement, we were in China about half of the time, and even rented an apartment there. After that for the next few years we would normally go for a few months out of the year. I was able to continue a teaching ministry in Mandarin to house church pastors and Bible school students. Ruth was able to continue her work to those affected by leprosy using both the Mandarin and Cantonese languages. This continued until 2020 when the devastating COVID plague broke out.

One of those years I taught in five different areas of China: the northwest, north-central, northeast, southwest, and the south. The course which I taught the most was 进 95/25 大门 ("Enter the 95/25 Big Door"), the Mandarin manual on cross-cultural ministry specializing in reaching Muslims with the gospel. At the end of this course is the faith plan: how many people will you teach the principles in the book to in the next twelve months? Their response has been most encouraging.

Ruth and I also enjoyed traveling together down the mighty Yangtze River several times, catching a steamship in Chongqing, where she had spent a couple years of her childhood, and sailing through the famous Three Gorges.

At the end of one of these trips, we needed to wait several hours before our train departed toward home, so we decided to walk around and take in some of the sights. As we came around a bend in the road, we noticed a building below us that had pointed windows like a church, so we walked toward to it. Upon entering the building, we saw that rooms had been constructed on either side of a central aisle. An elderly man greeted us and confirmed that it was indeed a church building. People had been living in the rooms there, but soon the church would reopen. He was the pastor.

A younger man came out to greet us and invited us into a side room to chat and have tea. The pastor came also, but he did not answer any of our questions. The younger man always answered, which seemed strange to us. Later, when the pastor was showing Ruth the pulpit area, I asked the young man about his work in the church. I was stunned by his reply. He was not a Christian. He was a Communist Party member assigned to reopen the church. I can only imagine how difficult that situation must have been for the old pastor. This, of course, was not a house church; it was a government-sponsored TSPM church.

SWITZERLAND

In 2015, Ruth and I celebrated our fifty-fifth wedding anniversary by taking a marvelous trip to Switzerland. Glenn had taken Polly there before, so he helped us plan our itinerary. He suggested we rent a car and drive to different places instead of going on tours. When we arrived in Zurich and tried to rent a car, however, we ran into a huge problem. In the United States, we commonly used credit cards for what we wanted. In Zurich, to rent a car, they demanded a debit card. We did not have one with us. What were we going to do?

Just then, who should appear at that exact place in the airport? A dear friend who traveled frequently for business, Scott McFarlane. We had not even known he was in Switzerland. We joyfully greeted each other and I told him my predicament. He let us use his debit card for the car rental security. How marvelous this was that it should happen at precisely the right place and precisely the right time! What a God-sent miracle!

I quickly adjusted to driving on the other side of the road like I had in Hong Kong, and we were on our way. We visited ancient castles, soaked in majestic mountain scenes, stayed in charming inns, appreciated the local culture, and enjoyed walking the beautiful trails of the Swiss Alps.

We rode Europe's highest mountain lift up to Glacier Paradise at 12,736 feet high. That deserved a kiss! The cable cars seemed suspended on perilously long cables. How wonderful to commemorate our many years together by enjoying God's creation!

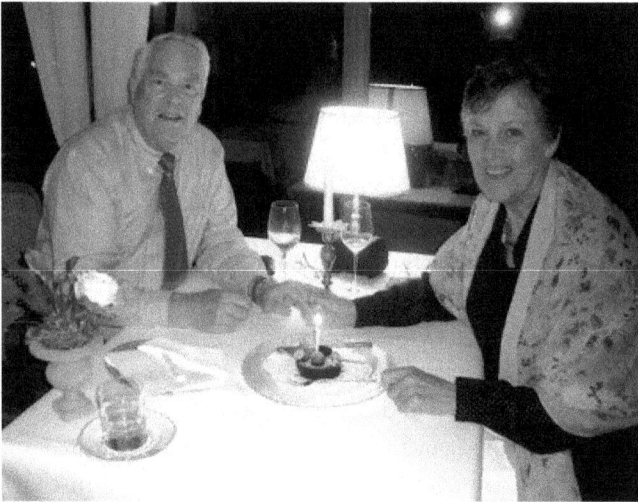

We celebrated our anniversary dinner at the marvelous Hotel Geissbach restaurant in Switzerland, in a beautiful setting near a sparkling mountain lake.

THE HOLY LAND

In 2017, Ruth and I had the privilege of taking a trip to Israel and Jordan. We had never been there before so this was a very special and meaningful experience. In Jordan, we stood on Mount Nebo where Moses stood and looked over the promised land before he died.

What a moving experience to visit the Garden of Gethsemane in Jerusalem. Our Heavenly Father allowed his one and only Son to go to the cross and die as atonement for our sins, and Jesus, who had never been separated from his Father, was willing to die for us. What unfathomable love is that!

"For God so loved the world that he gave his one and only Son, that whoever believes in him shall not perish but have eternal life. For

God did not send his Son into the world to condemn the world, but to save the world through him" (John 3:16–17).

I took the above picture of the Eastern Gate while standing at the garden of Gethsemane which faces it. This gate is also known as the Golden Gate and is a part of the wall of Jerusalem. The tip of the Dome of the Rock, an Islamic shrine built on the old Jewish temple site, is seen to the left. This Eastern Gate, now sealed, is where Jesus will enter Jerusalem when he returns to earth. He will first stand on the Mount of Olives, which is behind me on this side, and then enter the Eastern Gate (cf. Zech 14:4, 9; Ezek 43:1–7).

When we came to Capernaum by the Sea of Galilee, our excellent American tour guide told us that Jesus had performed more miracles there than any other place in Israel. We sat down inside the old Jewish synagogue, which was missing the roof but still had walls standing. He then gave us an invitation. "If anyone wants to come to me, I will pray for your healing. You can also go to [our local tour guide, a converted Arab, now a pastor] and he will pray for you."

I knew I had a physical problem. Before we had left on the trip, my resting heartbeat was too fast—120 to 130 beats per minute. We had decided to go anyway. Now I had a decision to make—should I ask for prayer or not? God already knew about my condition. It would not be anything new to him. I still hesitated as some went up to our American tour guide for prayer. I finally asked Ruth to come with me. "Let's go to the Arab pastor for prayer. No one else has gone to him." I explained my condition to him, and he prayed for me.

I did not know right away if anything had happened, but when we got back to Greenville after our trip, I checked my heart rate. It was in the sixties—what a miracle!

A BEND IN THE ROAD

In November 2017, Ruth and I visited family in China. We enjoyed days of games and fun with our grandchildren. One evening, I was out walking with the children around their neighborhood. "Try to catch us, Grandpa!" they dared me and took off running.

I could move pretty fast, though using a cane, so I took off after them. As I came to the road from the park my foot hit something and I fell down on one knee. The asphalt, from heavy vehicles, had been broken with one piece sticking up about one inch. I was wearing heavy jeans, so it did not hurt much. When I got back home, Ruth examined my knee. My jeans were not ripped and my knee only had a minor abrasion. It hadn't even bled. "Great, no worries!" I thought. But I was wrong.

I was scheduled to speak a couple days later on Sunday, and I was not feeling well, but felt I should keep the engagement. I sat in a chair while I spoke instead of standing like usual. I had train tickets for that afternoon to go teach at a Bible school for a few days. Several people thought I should not go, but I already had the tickets on an excellent fast train and felt I could rest on the train and feel better.

When I arrived at the Bible school, I discovered that their school building was under renovation. The temporary building they were using was cold and without central heating, so I kept all my layers of clothes on, even when sleeping.

My first day of teaching went all right, but when I walked into the classroom on the second day, my students became alarmed. There was no mirror in my lodgings, so I had not been able to see my face—it was all red, but I had not been outside under the sun. I had a fever and was put on the train immediately for home. By the time I got back to a warm place and took off my long johns and pants, the front of my leg from the knee down was bright red with infection.

It was difficult to get a bed in the hospital but finally it was worked out. I then continually received intravenous antibiotics, but for some reason they would not allow a doctor to operate on my leg and clean out the infection. It became very swollen and the infection was creeping up my leg.

As a general surgeon, my son Glenn had been carefully monitoring the situation from the United States. He became very upset because he knew my leg needed to be operated on to save my life. He called our travel medical insurance company in England and asked them to fly Ruth and me to Hong Kong. We had many friends in Hong Kong and were still resident citizens there, having gone back repeatedly after we lived there. Hong Kong had a very good hospital system with socialized medicine for their citizens. I could get an operation there immediately and time was of the essence. The insurance company finally agreed and arranged for a small ambulance plane to fly us there.

The air ambulance flew over from Taiwan to Mainland China to get us, returned to Taiwan to refuel, and then on to Hong Kong. It was tight quarters. There were two nurses and a doctor on the plane with us, but there was not even enough headroom to hang up the bags of IV medication the hospital had sold me before I left.

As Ruth began talking to the doctor she discovered he knew Cantonese language very well. How could this be? Taiwanese people speak Mandarin, not Cantonese.

She learned he was originally from Hong Kong and had attended grade school on the roof of an H-block building. "Could this possibly have been one of our church's two H-block schools?" she wondered. She said my Cantonese name, asking if he knew him. He thoughtfully repeated my name, then said, "Yes, I do know that name." He knew my name because he had been a student at our

H-block school! Of course, he had not realized it was me on the plane because many years had passed since then. What a tremendous blessing to discover that my doctor knew me on that plane. He encouraged Ruth to sleep. He would take care of me.

When we arrived at the Hong Kong airport, we did not taxi up to a gate like commercial planes. Once our plane stopped, they put me right into an ambulance which drove us straight to the Queen Mary Hospital where our Hong Kong friends had arranged for me to have the operation. The doctor from the plane generously also went with us to the hospital.

When we got there I was taken quickly to the operating theater. They found I had flesh-eating bacteria, necrotizing fasciitis, and it was red from way up my leg and way down. Without an operation I would die. Very soon two surgeons operated on me. The younger surgeon told me after the operation I had the most pus of anyone she had ever operated on, eight hundred cubic centimeters. Soon after I had another operation to put a skin graft over the open wound where they had cut away the infection.

Then began the long recovery period. For days, I lay in bed, unable to get up. Ruth, who was staying in a hotel nearby, would come to help me during the day and bring me special treats from McDonald's or Pizza Hut. I listened to audiobooks for hours with the excellent Bose headphones Glenn had given me.

When it was time to get up and start moving around, it was very difficult, even with a wheelchair. I cannot remember ever fainting in my life, except twice now, each for a very short time, when Ruth was pushing me in the wheelchair back to my bed.

I gradually improved enough to begin rehab and learn to walk again. When I first started, it hurt so much I felt like I was going to die. Things soon improved with the help of a good physical therapist. I began to walk again with a cane.

Glenn flew over from the United States after the surgery and spent several days encouraging us. He took Ruth out to see *The Phantom of the Opera* and a symphony concert, and wheeled me outside to enjoy some fresh air. Keith and his family also came to visit us during their Christmas break.

Including the rehabilitation period, I spent a total of around three months in the hospital. When we were finally ready to fly back to the United States, the insurance company arranged excellent tickets with seats that reclined into beds for both of us, and when we arrived in Chicago a chauffeured limousine took us on the long drive from the airport straight to our home Greenville.

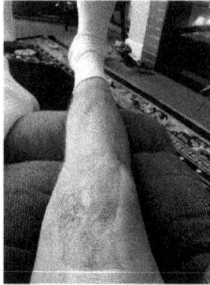

I have a long scar from the operations, but no matter; it sure looks better than before, and I am finally home!

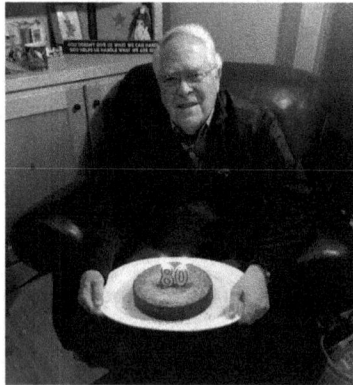

I was very thankful to be alive and to be able to celebrate my eightieth birthday on March 31, 2018, a couple months after that harrowing experience. "But those who hope in the Lord will renew their strength. They will soar on wings like eagles; they will run and not grow weary; they will walk and not faint" (Isa 40:31).

With my leg doing well, I was able to continue traveling. That June, I had the honor of performing the ceremony for our first grandchild who got married.

Here we are with our four sons at a family reunion in 2018; we are proud of each one of them. To my left is Dr. Mark Winslow, now senior vice president at Southern Nazarene University in Oklahoma City. On the far left is Dr. Keith Winslow, now a teacher in East Asia. To Ruth's right is Dr. Glenn Winslow, now a general surgeon in Great Falls, Montana. On the far right is Dr. Rodney Winslow, now associate superintendent of curriculum and instruction at Triad Community Public Schools in Troy, Illinois.

"Like arrows in the hands of a warrior are children born in one's youth. Blessed is the man whose quiver is full of them" (Ps 127:4–5a).

We now have four beautiful daughters-in-laws, eighteen grandchildren, and two great-grands.

The next spring, in March 2019, a few family members joined us on a trip to the high mountains of Costa Rica to see Ruth's older siblings, Margaret and Paul. We stayed in Margaret's beautiful Swiss-style house, explored the rainforest, and visited other beautiful sites including a butterfly habitat.

In the fall of 2019, Ruth and I took our last trip back to China. We took a cruise on the majestic Huangpu River in Shanghai. We still enjoyed each other after fifty-nine years of marriage!

For our sixtieth wedding anniversary, September 7, 2020, Ruth
fed me the first bite of cake like we did on our wedding day.

We got our miniature golden retriever pup, Jason (the name means "helper"),
in October 2021. He is my helper, most of the time. During the day, he keeps
me company downstairs where my office is, and in the evening, he hangs out
upstairs with Ruth and me. He is a great companion and gives us lots of joy.

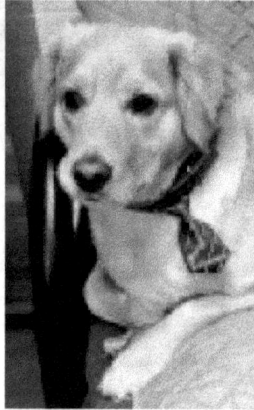

He is now more mature and knows a good number of words and hand signals. One favorite pastime is to run and bark furiously at any deer coming near our fence. He is a gentleman, yes, and loves everybody who comes into our house.

Now that I am old, I have been amazed at how God unexpectedly reveals knowledge about my physical condition which I did not know before.

In March 2022, three of our sons visited us in Greenville. When Glenn arrived, he wanted to surprise his brother, Mark, whom he had not seen for some time. Mark was sitting in my desk chair facing across the room as Glenn snuck up on him and prepared to give him a big slap on the shoulder. I was standing with my back to the desk just to the side of the chair. The whopping slap came, but it hit me instead of Mark—Glenn had slapped too soon! It was so sudden I had no time to prepare. I fell to the floor like a sack of potatoes, scraping my back hard against the sharp edge of my desk and hitting one of the brass knobs of a drawer on the way down. Of course it was an accident, but it developed into a large bruise on my right side that wrapped itself from my spine to the middle of my abdomen. Glenn wondered if I had broken a rib, which can be quite dangerous for a person my age. My doctor ordered chest X-rays and we were relieved to find that no ribs were broken.

The X-rays did, however, reveal that I had congestive heart failure. My heart was not pumping sufficiently, so fluid was building up in my lungs. One night I could not breathe, lying down in bed with my C-PAP machine. I had used this machine for years without any problems. I took it off, but still could not breathe right. I moved to my recliner chair in the living room and finally fell asleep. If I had not gotten that slap, I would not have understood my condition and not known what to do. Since then, I've started exercising more, and use a big pillow to elevate my head in bed, which helps me manage the situation better.

Fifteen years after retirement, in March 2023, the Greenville Free Methodist Church invited us to speak about our missionary work. They also wanted to celebrate Ruth's book, *Love Found a Way: The Journey of a Nurse in China.*

After we both spoke we were presented with some beautiful gifts. In the background hang quilts made by Ruth's Hands of Hope project in China.

Ruth and I celebrated our sixty-fourth wedding anniversary in September 2024 with a steak dinner grilled on our back deck. Ruth is my beautiful eighty-five-year-old wife, God's gift to me. Like the candle in front of her, she gives light by giving of herself. When I was a teenager in Taiwan, I used to go outside to look at the stars and think to myself, "The girl I will marry could be seeing these same stars now." God made it all happen!

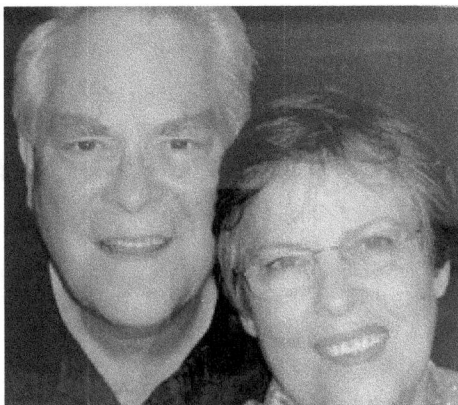

Ruth gave me a card many years before:

Dearest . . .
When I see you walking down the street in front of me . . .
When you catch my eye and no one else sees but me . . .
When you get me and give me a nice big kiss . . .
I know I just don't tell you enough how much you mean
to me . . .
So I got these two roses . . . and put them in this pretty
blue cup . . . my favorite color . . .
One is you and one is me . . . blooming so well togeth-
er . . . and touching.
Love always, Ruth

On the back of the card, I wrote with appreciation: "What a wonderful surprise to gladden my otherwise difficult day. Love you, Harry."

14

Senior Discernment

As I REFLECT ON life from the perspective of eighty-seven years, a few stories illustrate some important life lessons I learned along the way.

BICULTURAL PERSON

I am a 双文化的人, a bicultural person. By that I mean that when I am in China, I feel at home. I live among the Chinese people, not among foreigners. I speak their language, relish their food, appreciate their culture, and enjoy being with them. I not only feel at home. It *is* my home.

When I come back to America, I also feel at home. I live among Americans, speak English, relish the food, appreciate the culture, and enjoy being with them. I not only feel at home. It *is* my home.

To me, having two cultures is better than having only one. This is an important factor that helped sustain my journey in China for so long. I wasn't just "sticking it out." This was where God wanted me to serve him. I carried a curiosity and appreciation for the people and culture of both China and America, enabling me to serve with longevity and effectiveness.

LISTEN, DON'T TALK

My brother Paul taught me a helpful lesson: listen, don't talk. He was a top mechanic in the Robert Wesleyan College garage as a student there. He maintained and fixed the college cars, trucks, and tractors. He was so skillful he could fix almost anything with a gasoline engine. When I visited him as a young man, I had the privilege to be his "go-fer." I got him whatever tool he needed for what he was doing right then. He banged the lesson into my head, "Listen, don't talk. I am the mechanic. You are the go-fer." He would give the instructions. I needed to listen and follow carefully. It is a good trait to develop, and to this day I try to listen more than I talk.

One time, though, I did not listen with enough concentration to Paul. As an adult, he was a great motorcyclist. He and his two sons often won dirt bike races. On one visit to his home in Spokane, Washington, Paul offered to let me ride one of his dirt bikes. I hesitated because I had never even ridden a motorcycle before, let alone a dirt bike, but he explained how it worked and assured me I would be fine. He and some others would be riding on the same trail. I started out with them, but there was no way I could keep up with the experienced riders. I was going along slow but steady when suddenly, coming down a small incline, the bike toppled over on top of me! The motor was still running and the metal chain was still driving the wheel, now whirring in the air. I wondered for an instant if this would be my end. With a big effort, I pushed the bike away from me. Thankfully, I was not injured, except for a few bruises and my dignity, and I managed to ride the bike slowly back to the house.

Why had this happened? Paul had told me clearly, "When you go down an incline, do *not* use the front brake!" In the heat of the moment, that is exactly what I had done. I probably thought that using both the front and back brakes would slow me down faster. Instead, it caused a wreck. Why had I not listened more closely to Paul's instructions? I should have remembered the lesson he taught me many years before: listen, don't talk!

TRUST THE PILOT

One summer when I was visiting our farmer friend, Ervin Brown, at his home in Kansas, he asked if I would like to go for a ride in his small Piper Cub airplane. I was used to big jets and had never ridden in a small plane before, so I was curious about the difference. He took me up and showed me his farm from the air.

When we came back and were approaching the short grass runway, it looked to me like we were way too high to land. The runway was so close I thought we would overshoot it. "Aren't we too high to land?" I asked him. He answered, "Just watch me." He reached up over his head and turned a knob. We came down so smoothly and had a beautiful landing.

Trust the pilot—he knows what he is doing. Jesus is the only true pilot for our soul. If we believe in him, he will take us through the trials of life safely to heaven.

STICK WITH YOUR PARTNER

My sons Keith and Glenn are both avid scuba divers. Keith is even certified as a rescue diver and was a great help to me in passing my diving certification. Since we lived near Keith in Asia, we often went on diving trips together in different countries of that region. One of the first rules you learn is to always dive with a buddy.

I remember one time we went deeper than usual to see some shipwrecks. I could place my hands on two warships at the same time, one Japanese and one American. They were that close to each other at the bottom of the sea. We went so deep that I used too much air, so on the way back up I needed to buddy-breathe with our guide, sharing the air from his tank. Partway up, he directed me to extra air cylinders he had positioned for use closer to the surface so we could complete our five-minute safety stop there before surfacing. I was very thankful for such an experienced, well-prepared guide!

Another time, we dove down to a large ship which had an open door on the side of the hull. Our guide entered. Keith swam to the door and strongly motioned for me to come and then he entered. I was reluctant to go in, having never been inside a ship at the bottom of the sea before, but since they had both gone in, I decided I had better go, too. The three of us swam to a room that still had air trapped in it. What a surprise to pop our heads up into air that deep in the ocean! Next, we moved to the wheelhouse and pretended to be the captain of the ship. Lastly, we swam to the bow and had the tantalizing sensation of falling backwards off the boat. That whole dive was an unforgettable experience.

Another time, Keith and I went diving without a guide in a bay where the water was shallow for a long way before it deepened. We could follow long, narrow channels in the sand as we swam out. Before we left, Keith asked our guide how far we should go. "Go as far as you want; it is not deep." Since the sandy floor was fairly close, we could easily see a variety of small fish and other marine life as we swam slowly along. We went on and on and then suddenly realized it was getting dark and we were a long way from shore. Having our scuba gear on us, we decided swimming on our backs would be safer, though slower, than trying to swim under the water in the dark. It felt like a long time passed, but we finally saw a light shining in the distance. It was our guide, keeping a watch out for us. When we finally reached him, he told us he was just about to get into a boat and go look for us. We were glad to be safely back on dry land.

Sometimes we entered the water from the shore, but usually we jumped in from a boat. To gain proper buoyancy underwater, I wore weights on a belt around my waist. One thing divers soon realize is how inconvenient it is to go to the bathroom with a wet suit on. It's best to urinate in the water before you get back in the boat. One time I forgot to do that, and as the boat was not moving, I perched on the edge to jump back in the water to relieve myself. Before I jumped in, Glenn yelled, "Take off your weights!" If he had not warned me, I probably would have gone straight down to the bottom since I did not have any other equipment on to balance out the weights. To be safe, always dive with a buddy!

GRANDCHILDREN

In my experience as a grandparent, we sometimes found it difficult to know the moods of our grandchildren since we didn't see them daily. Here are two stories from babysitting a grandchild.

My son and his wife were speaking at a meeting. Ruth and I were at the back of the audience taking care of their two-year-old son. He sat quietly, without crying or wiggling too much. When the meeting was over, we pushed him in his stroller to a small restaurant nearby. So far, so good.

As he sat in a highchair waiting for the food to come, he began crying. It soon developed into screaming. We took him out of the highchair, but to no avail—he kept screaming. Other customers were eating nearby. This was getting embarrassing. I took him in my arms and walked away a bit, thinking this would be better. No way! He kept screaming. I placed him down on the floor. He then put his little hands on the floor, stretched out his legs, rolled his rump around in the air, and continued screaming as people were coming and going. This behavior was mortifying!

I quickly picked him back up and went to a secluded place. I had been telling him to be quiet, but he paid no heed. He just kept screaming. What was wrong with him? I carried him back to Ruth, still screaming, and she put him down in his stroller. He stopped screaming and fell asleep. Lo and behold, he was way too tired and we did not even know it.

Ruth and I were babysitting another grandson in his home while his parents were away. He was about five years old, having a great time in the bathtub with his toys. When it came time for him to go to bed, I asked him to get out of the bathtub. He said to me, "I don't have to obey you. You're not my dad." I calmly walked over to the door and turned off the light. He got out of the bathtub really quick!

WALK WITH HUMILITY

In early 2020, I had hip replacement surgery. Before my surgery, I used a cane when I went out of the house to public places. After the surgery, I used two canes because I had a problem balancing. I was reluctant to use a walker because I thought it might look bad. A doctor friend showed me a different perspective—when my friends see me with a walker, they are happy because they know I am safe. Other people who don't know me could care less. So why not use a walker?

After that good advice, I began using a walker in public places and at home. One great thing about the walker is that it provides four extra points of contact when you walk, where a cane only gives you one. When using a cane I had a very bad fall. I did not break anything, but I could not get up and we had to call 911. That was much more embarrassing than using a walker!

Another benefit I discovered about a walker is that people respect you and give you the right-of-way. Now you can find five walkers at my house: one for upstairs, one for downstairs, one for the deck behind the house, one in my car, and one in the garage for strolling walks and sitting on. I am literally the walker-walking man!

EMERGENCY ROOM

I do not like to go to the emergency room. It is too expensive! I have fallen down and my chair has tipped backwards, and I needed to call the 911 emergency crew to come help me up. After they get me up, they always ask if I want to go to the emergence room. I quickly decline their offer. One night not long ago, however, my answer changed.

That night I had a hard time sleeping and had trouble breathing. I took my C-PAP mask off, used my walker, and went to the living room recliner to see if I could sleep there, but I could not. I then went to the bathroom. When I turned with my walker to come out of the bathroom, I felt like my feet were lead. I could only move them a few inches at a time. What was the matter? I knew I had an irregular heartbeat, but I had never experienced anything like this before.

I called Ruth, but even with her help and the walker, I could not move my legs properly. I finally made it a few feet to the bedroom door and then collapsed, sliding down to the floor. What was the matter with me? Neither of us knew, but this time when the 911 crew came to get me up, I knew I had to go to the emergency room.

It was the first time I had been a patient in an ambulance. The technicians were efficient. At the emergency room, it was discovered I had pneumonia. They flew me by helicopter to a larger hospital, and there the doctor removed almost one and a half liters of water from my chest cavity. The water had been under my right lung, compressing it upward, which hindered my breathing. With breathing exercises, I gradually got my lung to expand downward so it would function normally again.

During this hospital stay, my cardiologist had me get a heart catheterization. It was an interesting procedure with big equipment, and I could see the surgeon performing it through a screen. They found I was all clear—no need for stents. Good to know!

Once I had recovered enough, I moved back to the hospital in Greenville where physical therapy nurses helped my legs to function better. I was in the two hospitals for a total of eighteen days, and then had a recovery period with physical therapy help at home.

Why did God allow this to happen? There are different answers to that question, but one certainly must be so that I would learn to have more patience. The Bible says, "Love is patient" (1 Cor 13:4), and "Whoever is patient has great understanding" (Prov 14:29). Another answer is that God did not want to take me to heaven before I finish writing this book. A third reason was to improve my health. I feel better now than before I had pneumonia, and now I know better how to keep my legs strong.

PHYSICAL BIRTH AND SPIRITUAL BIRTH

One December morning, our pastor reminded us that Mary was the real mother of Jesus, but Joseph was only his legal father (see Luke 1:26–35). Since Jesus was conceived through the power of the Holy Spirit, his real Father was God himself.

While reflecting on this, another amazing truth dawned on me. Although we who are Christians do not believe we are gods, which would be blasphemy, we do believe we are children of God and that God is our Father. "He came to that which was his own, but his own did not receive him. Yet to all who received him, to those who believed in his name, he gave the right to become children of God—children born not of natural descent, nor of human decision or a husband's will, but born of God" (John 1:12–13). There is a striking parallel between Jesus' physical birth and our spiritual birth. Both are accomplished through the power of the Holy Spirit. "He saved us, not because of righteous things we had done, but because of his mercy. He saved us through the washing of rebirth and renewal by the Holy Spirit" (Titus 3:5). Oh, the depth of the riches of God's grace, which we now only know in part!

WHEN THE TIME COMES

"But when the time had fully come, God sent his son, born of a woman" (Gal 4:4). Then when the time has fully come, God will again send his Son at the end of this present age. This time draws rapidly closer with multiple prophesies already having been fulfilled. When that time comes, those who believe in him will rise to be with him. Our physical bodies (then glorified bodies) and our spiritual bodies (our souls) will never die.

THE GUARDIAN ANGEL

"For he will command his angels concerning you to guard you in all your ways" (Ps 91:11). I appreciate the way the Chinese Bible puts this verse. 因他要为你分咐他的使者,

在你的一切道路上保护你 translates, "Because he will command his messengers to protect you on all your roads."

Not long ago, I was driving from Greenville toward St. Louis. I usually look over my shoulder to check for approaching trucks as I get on the interstate, but this time I forgot. My mind must have been on something else.

As I pulled onto the highway, I immediately saw in my mirror two big semitrucks neck and neck with each other barreling towards me, right on my tail. I was tempted to just step on the gas because my car was a hybrid with two motors and I knew it could take off like a rabbit, but the truck in my lane was far too close. In that split second, I pulled over to the shoulder of the highway. They thundered past, and I was safe.

How thankful I am for the angel who protected me that day! I am sure an angel has guarded me many more times than that.

THE CLEAR PAPERWEIGHT

On the desk where I work sits a paperweight. Four beautiful characters are inscribed on one side of the heavy, transparent, plastic cube: 事 主 蒙 福, which means "Serve the Lord, receive blessing." On the bottom of the weight under these characters, one corner of the cube has been cut off flat. It was not a mistake—there was a reason for that cut. When you carefully balance the cube on this flat corner, it sits at an angle so the characters face right up at you. It constantly reminds me that when I serve the Lord, I will receive blessings. Yes, blessings here and forevermore!

The painful sufferings of this life are like the corner cut off the paper weight. They often are not as terrible as you may think. Because of God's grace, they can even help you see him and reflect him more clearly. What a timeless wonder that is!

PART FIVE

Fellow Travelers

"Therefore, since we are surrounded by such a great cloud of witnesses,
let us fix our eyes on Jesus, the author and perfecter of our faith, who
for the joy set before him endured the cross."

(HEB 12:1A, 2A)

15

See You in Heaven

At times, when I traveled through the streets of China and looked at the people, I thought to myself, "They do not know anything about what God is doing in China." The following stories are just a few examples of the mighty work of God, who deeply loves the Chinese people. To protect the identity of these friends, I have changed their names.

BROTHER GEORGE

Some years ago, the People's Republic of China (PRC) was trying to influence the election of the top official in Taiwan. They wanted the leader to be a member of the Nationalist Party. They sent two missiles into the water near Taiwan, one at the north end and one at the south, trying to influence the election with a show of power. Near that same time, something miraculous happened inside Mainland China.

My good friend, Brother George, was traveling by train in China. He had rented a first-class sleeping berth since he was traveling through the night. His compartment had two bunk beds, but when he arrived, he was the only person there, so he took out his Bible and began to read. Suddenly, the door opened and a man in uniform entered. George could see that he was a high-ranking official, so he quickly put his Bible away.

Nothing happened though, so after a while George took his Bible out again to read. The officer saw it and asked, "Are you a Christian?" He replied, "Yes." The official went on, "My grandmother was a Christian." They began a wonderful conversation and George was able to clearly tell him who Jesus was. No other passengers came to sleep in their compartment that night to interrupt them. The result was the officer believed in Jesus, and went over and closed the drapes on the window in their compartment. "I want you to baptize me right here," he said, so George used tea from the glass on the small table under the window to baptize him. Before they parted, George gave his Bible to the officer to keep.

Who could have orchestrated that meeting but the mighty power of God which the world does not recognize? This is how God's kingdom grows in China.

BROTHER THOMAS

It was already dusk when Ruth, I, and a few others were climbing a trail winding up the mountain. We began to hear singing. It was ahead of us and, coming around a bend, we saw a small group of house church believers. We learned that they were singing a song one of the brothers present had composed. He shared with us the story of how he wrote it.

Brother Thomas had been to a house church in a town near a river. After preaching there, he left by boat to go to his next destination. He was greatly moved while standing on the deck as he looked back and saw how many believers had come to the shore to see him off, even though that was very risky. He kept watching them until he couldn't see them anymore. Then he wrote down a beautiful song commemorating this event. That was the song the Christians on the mountain were singing when we met them. I have translated the verses below.

Spiritual Brothers Are Much Closer Than Family Brothers
Spiritual brothers are much closer than family brothers,
Where is blood relationship deeper than spiritual relationship?
Together we receive the Lord's great love,
Together we receive the Lord's salvation,
Together we receive the Holy Spirit's leading,
Coming into contact we become one person. It's amazing!
Great salvation. It's hard to part with each other,
Loving each other, both being parts of the body,
Glorifying God the Father.

Spiritual brothers truly are closer than family brothers.
It is difficult for blood relationships
To be closer than spiritual relationships!
Together we live for one Spirit,
Together one family; we should obey the Holy Spirit.
Loving each other and being close to each other,
This great salvation of the Lord will not allow partition,
Being of the same mind, following the will of the Father,
Prospering the gospel.

Spiritual brothers indeed are closer than family brothers;
Blood relationships truly are not as close
As spiritual relationships.
Together we receive one promise,
Together we believe in one God,
Together we have one hope,
Waiting for the coming of the Lord,
Becoming one man through the Spirit,
Never departing from each other.
In unity, building the church,
Satisfying the heart of the Lord.

The life of the church needs unity;
Unity supplements the body of the Lord
Because the Lord gave his blood before,
Giving birth to the church.
He wants to call people according to his will—
True happiness!
Receiving the power of a king
Cannot be told completely.

When the time comes,
The door of grace has been shut,
It will be too late to be faithful.

What a beautiful time we had with Thomas and his fellow workers that night. He told Ruth and me the story below, one that he had told very few people before.

In 1976, Jiang Qing, Mao Zi Dong's wife, and three other top officials plotted to destroy Christianity in China. This group was so extreme and controlling that they had earned the nickname "Gang of Four."

Jiang Qing thought Christianity had been wiped out during the Cultural Revolution (1966–76). She boasted that they had put Christianity into a museum, but then she found out that Christians in a large house church movement were still meeting in secret. This time she plotted to smash it for good. The Gang of Four's plan was scheduled to start in the spring of 1976 and be completed within three years.

Their plan was simple. They would begin in Henan, the province which had the largest number of known Christians. They would first arrest and publicly interrogate three leading house church evangelists there and then execute them. Then they planned to round up other house church leaders and force them to denounce their faith. They thought if fear gripped the hearts of Christians, they would give up their faith, and as the campaign spread throughout China, Christianity would be destroyed. The church would be eradicated!

They schemed and began their plan, but it never came to completion. God intervened through a series of unexpected events in rapid succession in 1976, the very same year the Gang of Four planned to begin destroying the house church in China. Here is the sequence of events:

- January 8—Premier Zhou En Lai died.

- April 5—Riots broke out in Tiananmen Square.

- July 6—Field Marshall Zhu De died.

- July 28—A massive earthquake hit Tangshan, claiming an estimated 800,000 lives.

- September 9—Mao Zi Dong died.

- October 6—The Gang of Four themselves were arrested!

God is able to humble those who walk in pride!

Brother Thomas himself was one of the three leading house church evangelists in Jiang Qing's evil plan. He was arrested and put in prison in Henan. His interrogation and execution were to take place in the spring of 1976. The scheduled date came and passed but nothing happened. He still remained in jail.

Three other prisoners shared his cell. One day, those three were suddenly moved out and three new prisoners were brought in. One of them was a very high-ranking Communist Party secretary.

The next day Thomas heard his name being called from outside the cell and the guard threw a package in for him. Before he could pick it up the Party secretary grabbed it. "That is not your package," pointed out another prisoner. "I know, I know," he replied, but he kept holding it.

Thomas finally said, "You are being illogical! The package has my name on it. Why did you grab my package?" The Party secretary replied, "Truly, there is a God! Truly, there is a God! I accept defeat! I accept defeat!" Thomas realized something important was happening and silently prayed. Finally, he asked the man why he had said this. The Party secretary replied, "I could tell that you were not a local person, and when I saw your name, I knew it! I never thought I would be in here with you. Your life before was in my hand!"

Thomas asked him what the meaning of this was, and to his astonishment he found out this was the man the Gang of Four had used to have him arrested and put in prison! Their plan was to have him interrogated and executed! Now this man was in his very same cell. Thomas then had opportunity of sharing the gospel with this man who had scheduled his execution.

I had the privilege of meeting Thomas more than once. I will never forget the time he came with other brothers and sisters to meet us in a hotel room. We prayed together, kneeling in a circle. It felt like we were in heaven. When it was time for them to leave, I asked Thomas if I should go down with them on the elevator or stay in my room. He said I could go down. As the elevator descended, I said to him, "I do not know if I will get to see you again." He immediately replied, "We will see each other in heaven." He was right. I did not meet him again. He is now in heaven and I look forward to seeing him again there.

16

Everybody Sing

TODAY, IT IS EASY to find Christian music online, but in the late twentieth century, hymnals were even more scarce than Bibles among Christians in China. One research report stated that only one believer in a hundred possessed a hymnal.

Christians in China love to sing. Christians in the West also love to sing, but it is very different from what takes place in house churches. In American churches, songs are often about how God blesses us. In the house church, songs are more often about how we are to bless others—songs of faith and vision regarding our mission to share the gospel message. Songs based on Scripture are very common. House church preachers like to use Scripture songs while preaching their sermon. They suddenly begin a song and the audience joins in for the Christians have already memorized the song. Songs are also sung for personal devotions, and as a meaningful witness to non-saved relatives and friends.

In Chinese house churches, songs are sung in unison instead of four-part harmony like Western hymns. They are notated by the single-line, numbered musical notation system rather than the five-line staff with notes used in the West. You might think it would not sound as beautiful as four-part singing, but the passion and depth of heart with which they sing far make up for the missing harmony.

In the 1970s and eighties, Christianity spread like a wildfire throughout the countryside among poorly educated farmers. In cities and rural areas alike during the Cultural Revolution, schools closed and young people struggled to read. Add in the scarcity of printed materials and the animosity of the government in those days towards religion, and you can understand why the house church Christians relied on their memory and oral methods to learn Scripture. Combining music with Scripture made it even more memorable.

The song leader, usually a sister, would write words of a new song on the blackboard. She would sing a phrase while pointing at the words with a thin bamboo pole. With repetition, she would teach the audience, who caught on quickly, memorizing both the words and the tune. By the end, they could sing the new song by memory at home or with other Christians without needing a hymnal. I have always been amazed at the capacity for memorization of the Chinese people as shown in songs, the difficult writing system, the long national history, and the complex family terminology.

HANDMADE HYMNAL

Everybody Sing (大家歌唱), the hymnal used in the house church and described in chapter 11, developed in an unusual way. In the early 1980s, when Ruth and I were on a trip in China, I noticed a house church hymnal which had been produced there. Christians had laboriously created the hymnal on a hand-cranked mimeograph machine. After the sheets of paper were printed on one side, they were carefully folded and fastened together to make a book. The size was unwieldy—two inches thick, over five inches wide, and seven and a half inches long. It did not have a proper cover. Inside, it contained well over eight hundred hymns set to Chinese tunes, primarily composed of Bible verses.

I explained to the sister who had the hymnal that it could be reproduced on very thin paper at a fraction of this size, even small enough to fit inside a shirt pocket, like a book I had with me and showed her. This sister entrusted me with her precious mimeographed hymnal, which I still have.

RUTH LU

America had Fanny Crosby (1820–1915), who wrote over nine thousand hymns.[1] The sheer volume she wrote is amazing in its own right, but even more so when you learn that she was blind. We still sing many of her songs today.

China also has a very remarkable composer, Ruth Lu, who writes songs for house church Christians. A poorly educated farmer's daughter, Ruth had no formal training in music, but the Holy Spirit gave her a miraculous gift and she has written well over two thousand songs, some of which have been acclaimed by professional musicians for their craftsmanship.

On one trip in China, I was given a prized possession—a zippered, cloth-bound copy of Ruth's songbook called *Canaan Songs*. With 1,401 songs, you would expect it to be a very large book, but no, it was small enough to fit into a coat pocket. Here I have translated two beautiful, early songs by Ruth, which house church Christians love to sing. The first song includes sixteen names of our Lord and the second song has one line mentioned three times for strong emphasis. As they meditate on them and grasp their meaning, house church Christians find strength to face persecution and hope for the future amid hard circumstances.

The Rock the Rock Jesus Christ (*Canaan Songs* #77)
The Rock, the Rock, Jesus Christ,
Salvation is found in no one else.
There is no other name under heaven given to men.
Only you are the Savior, Lord.

You are the Son of Man,
You are the Mediator,
You are the Son of God,

1. Wikipedia, "Fanny Crosby."

You are the Lamb of God,
You are the Way,
You are the Truth,
You are Life,
You are Light.

The Rock,
The Fortress,
The City of Refuge,
The Shield.
We belong to you, and will never be shaken,
For ten thousand generations![2]

Preach the Truth Clearly (*Canaan Songs* #782)
Our generation is a blessed generation,
The harvest is already ripe, the Lord will soon come back.
Harvest workers, your work must not be shoddy,
Preach the truth clearly; make it understood.

When training workers, teach according to the Bible,
Pray, preach, and ask the Holy Spirit to send.
May our love have root and foundation,
Together understanding the Lord's love.

The hands of the clock already point to the last generation,
The harvest is already ripe, the Lord will come back.
Harvest workers, your work must not be shoddy,
Preach the truth clearly; make it understood.
Preach the truth clearly; make it understood.[3]

Later I had the great privilege of meeting Ruth. I was deeply honored to be asked by coworkers to pray for her. She had read one of our manuals, *Enter the 95/25 Big Door*, mentioned in chapter 11, which is about reaching Muslim people with the gospel. God inspired her to write two songs about this. I have translated the Chinese lyrics below.

2. *Canaan Songs*, 65–66.
3. *Canaan Songs*, 511.

We Will Continue Along This Road (*Canaan Songs* #1331)
We will continue along this road.
The vision becomes ever more clear.
We will go in faith over vast deserts,
With the pillar of cloud by day,
And the pillar of fire by night.

We will continue along this road.
We definitely will not turn back
From this which is our heart's desire.

The camel train has already stepped out
On to the long journey west,
Slowly going over the sand dunes
Without any hindrance.

The Lord has already opened
The road to the west.
This is our vision
And the Lord's commission.

We follow the example of our forefathers,
With trials and hardship coming at double pace.
Suffering, however, is a blessing.
The Lord will at all times be our help.[4]

God's Special Attention to Ishmael (*Canaan Songs* #1334)
There is a people group,
Who has received God's special love,
The descendants of Ishmael.

Their numbers have increased greatly up to now,
And they live everywhere.
They do not yet know Jesus,
And still live in darkness.
Quickly ask the Lord to bring them,
Back to the tents of Abraham.

---

4. *Canaan Songs*, 925.

Ishmael and Isaac were blood brothers.
Both received precious promises,
From the Heavenly Father.
There have been great upheavals,
And enemy attacks.
This hatred must not continue.
Ask God to send our brothers and sisters,
To them where they are.

Ishmael and Isaac were blood brothers.
The time will come,
When they will come back together in Christ.

Ishmael and Isaac were blood brothers.
The time will come, when they will come back together.
This is the will of God.[5]

---

5. *Canaan Songs*, 928.

17

Of Whom the World Is Not Worthy

LORA WAS A CHINESE citizen all her life. Edith was a single American missionary who adopted Lora. Geneva was another single American missionary. Mark Ma was a Bible school teacher who received a special vision from God. They all are now in heaven. "The world was not worthy of them" (Heb 12:38a).

LORA JONES

In the early missionary groups, children of different families often played together as cousins and called all the other parents "aunt" or "uncle." I thus considered Lora as a cousin, for she was the daughter of Edith Jones, who was in the same mission as my parents. Lora may have heard about me from her mother, but she was not where my parents were when I was a little boy in China.

Over the decades, I would hear snippets of news about Lora, but then marvelously Ruth and I were able to visit her in November 2012 in Lanzhou in Northern China. What a tremendous privilege to finally meet her! We asked her many questions about her own life and her mother, Edith.

The following stories come from various sources including our conversations with Lora, Ruth's research at our Free Methodist church's historical library in the United States, Back to Jerusalem accounts, and my mother's book *Tomorrow*.

Ruth and Lora are holding *Tomorrow*, which has a beautiful picture of Lora on the cover.

On a cold March day in 1914, a little bundle of cloth was left at the city gate. A man passing by picked it up and discovered a tiny baby girl inside. She was taken to Edith Jones, who raised her as her own child. Edith gave her the English name Lora and the Chinese name 爱喜 *Ai Xi*, which means "Love's Delight," because she loved her so much.

Lora attended Chinese school in her hometown and then continued her studies at a Christian high school near Shanghai. When it was time for college, Edith arranged for her to attend Greenville College. She spent two years there before transferring to Seattle Pacific University for her final two years.

After graduation, Lora could have stayed in the comfort and safety of America during WWII. Instead, she chose to return to

China to help her mother care for orphans in Northern China. It was a horrendous trip. She traveled with a lady nurse who was in the same mission as her mother. It was too dangerous to go across the Pacific by ship during the war, so they flew to Argentina, then by boat to Africa. Next, they sailed to India where they flew across the Himalayas to Chongqing in China. The final leg of their journey was a nine-day road trip by truck.

> This was a wild ride, but a beautiful one. The country was rugged, with steep hills and sharp curves. From this mountainous road they could see terrace fields, waterfalls, rice fields, numerous trees and flowers. . . . As they chugged along those mountain roads, often very close to precipitous cliffs, many times they lifted their hearts to God for their safety. When they were near their journey's end, just as they were going down a steep hill, the brakes would not hold. When the emergency brake was used, it began to smoke and burn. The car was finally stopped. The two ladies were sitting in the front seat. Suddenly the nurse noticed that her foot was getting warm. Looking down, she saw flames shooting up. They jumped out of the car.[1]

God protected them and they finally arrived at the mission station only to find out that Edith had moved to another province. Lora embarked once more, but it was worth the effort for the joyful reunion when she finally saw her mother again.

EDITH JONES

Lora also shared with us the amazing story of what Edith had been through before they reunited. It is similar to the legendary Gladys Aylward story told in the book *The Small Woman* and the movie *The Inn of the Sixth Happiness*. Edith's story has not been publicized like Gladys' was, but it clearly shows God's care for his own children.

During the Sino-Japanese War in the late 1930s, Edith, with the school principal and several teachers, walked for many days with

---

1. Winslow, *Tomorrow*, 111.

eight hundred orphans heading for relative safety in Northern China. The route was filled with danger and hardship for they had to march a good number of miles a day to keep ahead of the advancing Japanese army in rough terrain and exposure to the elements.

One day, soldiers from a nearby town came and pointed their guns at Edith, demanding she give them money. They knew she must have money from an aid agency to buy food for so many orphans on their long journey. Edith gave them the money. Back in town, an influential Chinese man went to the soldiers' superior and explained to him that the money they stole was intended to buy food for eight hundred orphans. "Please do not let them starve!" he entreated. The army officer ordered the soldiers to give the money back to Edith. They did give most of it back and the orphans did not starve.

Edith was sixty-seven years old when she walked west with the orphans. They walked slowly because many of the orphans were young children. When Japanese planes flew overhead, they would scatter into the fields, quickly hunching down to hide. It's not easy to hide a group of eight hundred children! When they finally arrived in Xi'an, capital of Shannxi Province, with ragged clothes and sore feet, an organization gave them all new clothes to wear. That was where Lora reunited with her mother, having just finished her grueling, circuitous route from the United States. Edith died six years later at the age of seventy-three.

I asked Lora regarding a story I had heard about her mother and robbers. They came looking for money. The money was in one of the trunks Edith had. She sat on the trunk and would not get up. The robbers, not finding the money, finally left. Lora told us she had not heard this story. She remarked earlier to us her mother did not speak much.

After returning to China, Lora joined a sewing class offered in a church. Soon she obtained a sewing machine and used her skills to make whatever clothes she wanted. In the late fifties Lora was incarcerated by the Communist Chinese government. Edith was already in heaven. At that time there was little food to eat. She was put to work in a factory making clothes where they could watch her. Some of her young orphans were able to come and visit her and fortunately she had enough to eat.

Lora was incarcerated for her faith and previous connection to foreigners. Outside the factory, millions of Chinese people were dying of famine. If Lora had been sentenced to hard labor on a farm instead of a factory, she could have died from starvation. The skills she had learned in the church became the key for her survival during this difficult period.

The cadres did not tell her how long she would have to stay. They claimed she was a spy for America. She told them she was not that intelligent. They claimed she was against the revolution. She told them she preached the gospel. They then proclaimed that it was "thought ideology."

Lora took great care to do her sewing well. Realizing her diligence, they assigned her to check the quality of other workers' sewing. The factory supplied military uniforms, and they had to be made correctly.

Because she was given more responsibility, Lora had to attend indoctrination meetings led by a cadre in the afternoons and by a section leader at night. The night sessions were the worst. Physical torture was administered on those who resisted or disagreed with the teaching. They were beaten, and some were made to carry a beam on their shoulders. Lora, as the head of her small group, called for a doctor to help a lady in her group who had been beaten. Others criticized her for giving aid to someone who was being "corrected." Those were long, hard years, but she was sustained by the word of God. She had memorized Pss 23, 27, and 91:11–16.

After ten years, Lora was given permission to go home, but she did not have a home to go to. Her home had been in the church, but the church had been closed. Lora was then taken to work in a hospital owned by the police. She was assigned to do laundry. Ten more years passed. She was finally released at the end of 1979.

For thirty years, none of Lora's friends in the United States had heard any news from her. They didn't know if she was dead or alive. After being released from her laundry assignment, one of her previous students gave her a Christmas card and asked if she knew a certain missionary who had lived in China before the war. Lora recognized his name and was able to get his address. How her friends rejoiced when they finally got news from her! Later, Lora was able to visit some of them in the United States for a short time.

Lora died at the age of 105. God's faithfulness had carried her through prison labor, famine, loneliness, and persecution, but she was *Ai Xi*, "Love's Delight," and her Heavenly Father loved her very much.

**Lora Jones and Pastor Mark Ma visited each other
in May 2008. Both are now in heaven.**

MARK MA

When Ruth and I met Rev. Ma in China some time ago he said to me, "I want you to meet my son, because your mother gave the baby basket she had used for you to us so we could use it for our son on our long trip north." They were going from Henan Province in Eastern China all the way to Shanxi Province in North China. The reason for that trip was to help James Hudson Taylor II to begin a Bible school there, outside of Japanese-occupied China. Rev. Taylor would be the principal and Rev. Mark Ma would be the vice principal. The school was organized and began successfully. Sometime later, after the school was well established, a truly remarkable thing happened. God gave Mark a charge to go west and preach the gospel through Muslim countries all the way to Jerusalem. Mark argued with God, contending that other Christians outside of China should do this, but God revealed to him that he was to go. God wanted to give that section of the world as a spiritual inheritance to the Chinese church.

God began a mighty move among the students and teachers. They held a special vision-casting meeting. The students were told that in the courtyard different provinces of China had been drawn with chalk on the ground. The students were to stand in the province they felt God was leading them to go to and preach the gospel. A number of students went and stood in Xinjiang, now known as the Xinjiang Uyger Autonomus Region.

Xinjiang was famous for the ancient Silk Road trade route which began in Eastern China, extended all the way through Xinjiang, and continued west across Central Asia until it finally entered the important cities of the Middle East, including Jerusalem.

From that vision-casting meeting and much prayer before and after, God moved Rev. Ma and others to form the "Preach Everywhere Evangelistic Band." Their vision was to go west to preach the gospel in Muslim villages in China along the Silk Road and then outside China all the way back to Jerusalem. Missionaries who knew what was happening called this the "Back to Jerusalem Evangelistic Band."

What does "Back to Jerusalem" mean? Throughout history, the gospel moved in a generally western direction, from Israel through Europe, across to the Americas, then to China. But Central Asia, with its many Muslim countries, had largely been neglected. The gospel must be preached west all the way *back to Jerusalem* where it started.

The Preach Everywhere Evangelistic Band set out heading west along the old Silk Road in China. Transportation was very difficult in the rough terrain. They rode camels in the great desert sand dunes. Sometimes they walked from place to place. Along the way, they preached in Muslim villages. It took a long time, but some of them finally made it to Kashgar at the western edge of Xinjiang near Kyrgyzstan. You can imagine their frustration and dismay when they found out they were not allowed to leave China to continue their mission. China's government had changed hands and the newly-in-charge Communists had closed all the borders, prohibiting people from leaving.

Mark and the other evangelists never forgot the vision God gave them to carry the gospel west, but its fulfillment would wait for a later generation to pick up the baton and carry it forward. This early vision still burns brightly in the heart of the house church of China today.

Pastor Mark and his friends could never have imagined the amazing transformation that is taking place along the old Silk Road today.

> The Belt and Road Initiative (BRI or B&R), known in China as One Belt One Road and sometimes referred to as the New Silk Road, is a global infrastructure development strategy adopted by the Chinese government in 2013 to invest in more than 150 countries and international organizations. The BRI is composed of six urban development land corridors linked by road, rail, energy, and digital infrastructure and the Maritime Silk Road linked by the development of ports. . . ."Belt" refers to the proposed overland routes for road and rail transportation through landlocked Central Asia, along the famed historical trade routes of the Western Regions; "road"

is short for the 21st Century Maritime Silk Road, which refers to the Indo-Pacific sea routes through Southeast Asia to South Asia, the Middle East and Africa. It is considered a centerpiece of Xi Jinping's foreign policy. . . . As of early 2024, more than 140 countries were part of the BRI. The participating countries include almost 75% of the world's population and account for more than half of the world's GDP.[2]

The BRI makes travel to Muslim countries between China and Jerusalem so much easier. Now is the time to fulfill the "Back to Jerusalem" commission God gave to the Chinese church a generation ago. Young Christians in China are catching the vision, responding to the call, and preparing to head west. May God give them the opportunity to receive cross-culture missionary training before they go, like in the manual *Enter the 95/25 Big Door* (进 95/25 大门). Then may God send them forth to reach multiple ethnic groups along the New Silk Road so they can come to know and believe in the Creator of the universe. Jesus said, "I am the way and the truth and the life. No one comes to the Father, except through me" (John 14:6).

GENEVA SAYER

Geneva Sayer was the last missionary of our Free Methodist church to leave China after the Communist government came to power. She was under house arrest for her last two years. She could have returned to the United States after that ordeal. Instead, she was the first Free Methodist missionary to move to Taiwan, where she began to plant churches. I met her when I arrived in Taiwan as a teenager with my mother, who had been appointed as the next missionary to help in the work.

I will never forget how Geneva loved to sing one particular verse of Scripture in Mandarin with a Chinese tune. "If we live, we live to the Lord; and if we die, we die to the Lord. So, whether we live or die, we belong to the Lord" (Rom 14:8). Geneva liked to say

2. Wikipedia, "Belt and Road Initiative."

"I" instead of "we" in the Mandarin song as she sang so it would mean, "Whether I live or die, I still am the Lord's." Geneva was an inspiration to many people!

Epilogue

I WROTE THIS POEM.

A Poem
I am a tool in my Master's hand.
He bought me. I belong to him.
He fashioned, shaped me for his use.
I rejoice how he used this tool.
All praise, honor, and glory are his.
Both now and forever.

This song impacted my life:

A Song
Wonderful Grace of Jesus,
Greater than all my sin;
How shall my tongue describe it,
Where shall its praise begin?
Taking away my burden,
Setting my spirit free,
For the wonderful grace of Jesus reaches me.

Wonderful the matchless grace of Jesus,
Deeper than the mighty rolling sea;
Higher than the mountain,
Sparkling like a fountain,
All sufficient grace for even me;
Broader than the scope of my transgressions,
Greater far than all my sin and shame;

Oh magnify the precious name of Jesus,
Praise His name![1]

A profound verse that helped me:

A Verse
Trust in the Lord with all your heart
And lean not on your own understanding;
In all your ways acknowledge him,
And he will make your paths straight.
(Prov 3:7)

A PEN NAME

My parents are buried next to each other in the Oakwood Cemetery in Warsaw, Indiana.

Mother had 明 "clear" and 天 "sky" engraved on my father's gravestone. These two characters together actually mean "tomorrow." Mother eventually titled her book about their experiences in China *Tomorrow*.

---

1. Lillenas, *Hymns of Faith and Life*, no. 106.

I had 燿 "brilliance" and 光 "light" engraved on Mother's gravestone. Later, I took one character from each of my parents' gravestones to create a meaningful Chinese pen name for myself, 明燿 *Ming Yao*. Putting these two characters together means "clear brilliance" and reminds us who believe in Jesus of our eternal home, the Holy City of Jerusalem: "It shone with the glory of God, and its brilliance was like that of a very precious jewel, like a jasper, clear as crystal" (Rev 21:11).

AN APPOINTMENT

When I get to heaven, after I meet my Savior Jesus, I want to meet close family members there. There is one special person I want to spend extra time with since I did not get to do so on earth. That is my dad, Harold Hezekiah Winslow, who went to heaven when I was six years old. Jesus said: "I am the resurrection and the life. Whoever believes in me, though he die, yet shall he live" (John 11:25 ESV).

AN ETERNAL DECLARATION

I close this book with three of the most profound statements of all time:

Epilogue

"The heavens declare the glory of God; the skies proclaim the work of his hands. Day after day they pour forth speech; night after night they display knowledge" (Ps 19:1–2).

"For God so loved the world that he gave his one and only Son, that whoever believes in him shall not perish but have eternal life. For God did not send his Son into the world to condemn the world, but to save the world through him" (John 3:16–17).

"For thine is the kingdom, and the power, and the glory, for ever. Amen" (Matt 6:13b KJV).

I pray these last two words, *"for ever,"* in the Lord's Prayer will ring clearly in your heart. Are you in his kingdom? Do you know him as your Heavenly Father?

Bibliography

The 1955 Morrisonian. N.p., n.d.

The 1956 Morrisonian. N.p., n.d.

Lillenas, Haldor. "Wonderful Grace of Jesus." In *Hymns of Faith and Life*, hymn number 106. Winona Lake, IN: Light and Life, 1976.

Wikipedia. "Belt and Road Initiative." November 17, 2024. https://en.wikipedia.org/wiki/Belt_and_Road_Initiative.

———. "Fanny Crosby." November 1, 2025. https://en.wikipedia.org/wiki/Fanny_Crosby.

Winslow, Carolyn V. *By Love Compelled: Life Story by Carolyn Winslow.* Winona Lake, IN: Light and Life, 1981.

———. *China's Four Sons.* Winona Lake, IN: Light and Life, 1965.

———. *Tomorrow.* 3rd printing. Winona Lake, IN: Light and Life, 1946.

Winslow, Ruth. *Love Found a Way: The Journey of a Nurse in China.* Indianapolis: Light and Life, 2021.

———. *The Mountains Sing: God's Love Revealed to Taiwan Tribes.* Winona Lake, IN: Light and Life, 1984.